ANDRÉ DERAIN

PHAIDON

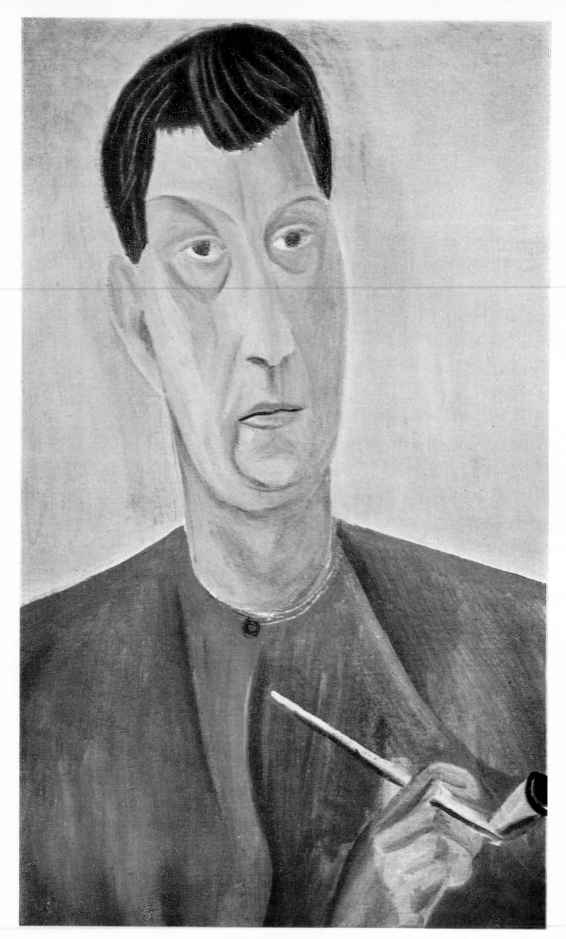

SELF-PORTRAIT. 1914

ANDRÉ DERAIN

BY DENYS SUTTON

WITH ONE HUNDRED ILLUSTRATIONS
INCLUDING TWENTY-FOUR
IN FULL COLOUR

PHAIDON PUBLISHERS INC
DISTRIBUTED BY DOUBLEDAY AND COMPANY INC
GARDEN CITY · NEW YORK

THE PAINTINGS OF ANDRÉ DERAIN ARE REPRODUCED
BY ARRANGEMENT WITH ASSOCIATION POUR LA DIFFUSION
DES ARTS GRAPHIQUES ET PLASTIQUES · PARIS
© PHAIDON PRESS LTD · LONDON · 1959
PRINTED BY GEO. GIBBONS LTD · LEICESTER
MADE IN GREAT BRITAIN

CONTENTS

ANDRÉ DERAIN

MANY good judges of artistic form in the years just before and just after the first world war considered Derain to be a leading, if not the leading, member of the French *avant garde* and the main upholder of the national tradition—the successor, in short, to the great masters of the previous century. But all this was to change and, at the close of his life, he was to many, including some of his former admirers, little more than a discredited and half-forgotten figure, one who had been outpaced by events—the recluse of Chambourcy, the odd man out even of the 'heroic' generation of the 1900s.

An explanation, however summary, of the reasons which prompted so much critical opinion to turn against his art is by no means easy, and it ought not to be overlooked that the artist's own indiscretion in visiting Germany while France herself was occupied contributed not a little to the hostility which he provoked. The reluctance of modern criticism to reckon with Derain may be attributed to another reason: the belief, so firmly held in our own time, that 'originality', *per se* and in its most obvious forms, is the principal measuring rod applicable to an artist's work, one that automatically operates even if he himself declines to accept the premises on which such a view is based. Derain, it is often maintained, was a true painter and a creative artist only during that time, a relatively short one in respect of the age at which he died, when he was overtly an experimental one: that is to say, during the years from 1900 to 1914, when he was one of the principal exponents of Fauvism and in close touch with the Cubists.

But is this interpretation of his contribution, attractive owing to its very simplification, substantiated by the facts? Did his painting lamentably and sadly fall off in the years after the first world war or, for all his alleged espousal of 'reactionary' artistic principles, did it still contain qualities calling for praise rather than condemnation? In this connection, his art ought to be assessed in terms of his own precepts and aims rather than in those of its relevance to preconceived notions determined by an arbitrary and didactic conception of art. What counts in such matters is the intrinsic value of each canvas and not its relationship to the style of the moment, or rather to that style which has gained currency, rightly or wrongly, as holding that position.

At crucial moments in his career, his rejection of some of the major currents of the day—Cubism and Abstraction, for instance—did not stem from a drying up of his inspiration and from an inability to venture in these directions, even if he had so desired; it was the consequence of a reasoned personal point of view. He was surely entitled to paint in any way he wished, so long as the result answered to, and reflected, his own preoccupations. The technical ability

5

and artistic quality of many (though by no means all) of those later works which are often despised must likewise indicate that he chose the route he did because he realised—and who better?—that it suited him. His courage and integrity were manifest in his determination to adhere to his position and to pursue his own star; he absolutely refused to trim his sails in favour of fashion.

The assessment of his art is still a complex matter, and the student, anxious to follow the various stages of his stylistic evolution and to gauge the import of his theories, hermetic and paradoxical though these may sometimes prove, is at a disadvantage. Whereas the majority of the leading painters of his generation—a Picasso, a Braque, a Matisse—have been before the public for many years, forming the subjects of special or general studies and of innumerable exhibitions in many countries, this is not the case with Derain. Nearly all the books or essays dealing with his work appeared some thirty years ago, when he was still the lion of the Parisian scene. Moreover, the artist himself refrained from exhibiting during the latter part of his life. Thus, although several exhibitions of his work have been staged since his death, the precise sequence of his stylistic development is still partly obscure: and speculations on this all-important point are rendered still more difficult owing to the rarity of dated pictures by him. For this reason any account of Derain, as man and artist, ought to endeavour to particularise the principal stages of his evolution, especially in the years before the first war when he drew close to, and then drew back from, the contemporary revolutionary movement.

DERAIN was born on the 10th June, 1880, at Chatou, a charming small town lying on the Seine, to the west of Paris, a sort of Barbizon, as he once termed it, which was singularly rich in motifs likely to appeal to a painter. His father was a prosperous pastry cook and a municipal councillor, and, as a youth, Derain seems to have been called upon to help with the family business as a delivery boy. After attending the school of Sainte-Croix at Le Vésinet, he went to the Lycée Chaptal in Paris and there, in 1895, he carried off a prize for drawing and another for natural science. His parents, who were evidently ambitious for him, intended that he should become an officer or an engineer, and as a step in the fulfilment of these aims, he was sent to the Ecole des Mines in Paris.

However, Derain soon turned to painting and when about fifteen he received some lessons from 'le père' Jacomin, whose son was a member of his class at school. Jacomin, although knowing Cézanne, detested his painting, and Derain later avowed that he probably gained nothing from this instruction; all the same, by accompanying his mentor and his son on their expeditions to paint the local scene he was introduced to a branch of painting in which he was subsequently to excel. His artistic ambitions were doubtless nourished, and his intellectual appetite stimulated, by the friends he made in Paris, and these included the son of Villiers de l'Isle-Adam, the symbolist poet, Linaret, a fellow-painter, and the Comte de la Noé, a young eccentric Breton aristocrat whose influence on a sixteen-year-old student Derain gratefully acknowledged after his companion's premature death in 1902.

Like other neophytes of the period, Derain soon found his way to the Académie Camillo in the Rue de Rennes in Montparnasse where Eugène Carrière, the dreamy symbolist painter with radical political ideas, whom Derain later described as being 'very intelligent', occasionally dropped in to give some casual teaching. It was there that he came across Henri Matisse, then in his early thirties, and already a leader of the younger set. Although Matisse was clearly aware of 'the serious, scrupulous work of this highly gifted artist' (Derain) and Derain was later to admit that from about 1900 a 'kind of Fauvism' was evident in Matisse's painting, such of Derain's work as survives from this period indicates that he was hardly a proto-Fauve like his elder colleague.

His first works, in fact, are reported to have been landscapes after the manner of Corot but one of the few dated painting from these days, *The Road to Carrières* of 1899 (Fig. 2), with its use of flat passages of colour and the almost synthesist treatment of the sky, suggests a possible awareness of Cézanne and Gauguin. There is no evidence available on this point, but he may well have already seen Cézanne in Paris while he visited St. Michel-en-Grève in Brittany in 1898 and may have encountered work by the School of Pont-Aven in this region or in Paris. The early *Self-Portrait* (Fig. 1), although containing certain characteristics of Derain's later style, notably the fluent handling of the rim of the bowl in the still life, also suggests a touch of Cézanne. On the other hand, *The Funeral* (Fig. 3), which is datable to about 1899, indicates his appreciation of Manet as well as his affection for those animated figures which subsequently often appeared in his painting. Above all, Derain had now embarked on a close study of the Old Masters in the Louvre and while working there he again met Linaret, then copying Uccello in this museum.

A significant change in his life occurred as a consequence of his friendship with Vlaminck. Although previously known to each other by sight, they met only in July 1900 when a train in which they were travelling from Chatou to Paris was involved in a crash. They took to each other at once, as well they might; for Vlaminck, who was several years older than Derain and had only just finished his military service, was a heady and stimulating companion. Painting by day he earned his living by playing at night as a gipsy violinist in such places as the Petit Casino de Montmartre, the Café des Princes and with the Marchetti band at the first motor show. An angry young man of the era, like so many artists and writers of the day, he was a fervent anarchist, a supporter of Dreyfus and a contributor of poems and prose to such reviews as *L'Anarchie* and *Libertaire*, and, as was to be expected, he was immersed in the writings of Zola, Kropotkin, Marx, the Goncourts and Le Dantec. Virtually untrained as a painter, his *Man with a Pipe* (*Le Père Bouja*) of 1900, belonging to Madame Vlaminck at Rueil-la-Gadelière, presents gnarled, contorted features painted with a violence reminiscent of Monticelli or Van Gogh.

Derain's parents, careful and comfortable bourgeois of *la belle époque*, strongly disapproved of their son's friendship with a Bohemian and anarchist like Vlaminck. If the stories retailed by his companion are to be taken at their face value, the two friends shocked the inhabitants of Chatou by their behaviour—as when they returned from Montmartre after an evening out ostentatiously mounted in a fiacre in the company of two prostitutes decked with distinctive boas. Such escapades, hardly surprising for two highly spirited and energetic young men, did not prevent them from working hard, and in the winter of 1900-1901 they installed themselves in an old restaurant, the Hôtel Levanneur, on the island at Chatou, between the two bridges, and there, as he later recalled, Derain once saw 'Degas, on a boat on the Seine, wearing a heavy fur coat in August.'

There too, the young men painted and received their friends—de la Noé and his mistress, Paulette, who after his death decamped with Octave Mirbeau, the novelist and critic, Champenois, who worked in an insurance company, and Lucien Grillet, an architectural student. On such occasions, conversation turned on the controversies of the day and they discussed the anarchist and naturalistic writers or Cézanne and Courbet and the 'primitives'. It was the passion for the radical, which formed the theme of their talk, that induced Vlaminck, eager to defy the past, to use pure, primary colours in his pictures, with the result that he and Derain brought back with them what he termed 'canvases completely daubed with violent colours, vermilion and yellow', and in these early, happy days Derain spoke of them as being 'always drunk with colour, with words which speak colour, and with the sun which imparts life to colour'.

The extent to which this discovery of pure colour and concern for light was translated into Derain's own compositions at this point is still relatively obscure, and the *Self-Portrait* (Mme Alice Derain, Chambourcy) which has been variously dated 1900 and 1905, but which seems to belong to the earlier, rather than the later, period, and *A Corner at Chatou*, 1900 (Private collection, Paris), for all their brio, strike something of an air of melancholy. All the same, his taste for bold and startling colour was evident enough in two of his Chatou landscapes, probably painted in 1901 (formerly with the Valentine Gallery, New York, and with Ambroise Vollard), with their simplified formal structure and even more so in the expressionistic copy of *Christ carrying the Cross* (Kunstmuseum, Berne), then attributed to Benedetto Ghirlandajo, which was painted in 1900-1901. In this work he considered it 'necessary not only to put colour on again but to accentuate the expression'.

SELF-PORTRAIT. About 1912

MADAME DERAIN IN A WHITE SHAWL. About 1919-1920

Derain's friendship with Vlaminck, his fruitful contacts with some of the more go-ahead artists like Othon Friesz, whom he met in 1901, and his sharp interest in intellectual matters, quickly brought him into touch with a wider circle. He had even begun to earn some pocket money by contributing drawings to the Parisian press under the signature of *Bouzi*. In these exciting times, a series of important exhibitions, mainly held at the art dealers' galleries, enabled an inquisitive young painter to study the major masters of the nineteenth century, and the array of Van Gogh's paintings shown at the Bernheim-Jeune gallery in 1901, came as a revelation to Derain and many of his contemporaries. And it was on this occasion that he introduced Matisse to Vlaminck.

'I saw Derain,' Matisse wrote, 'in the company of an enormous young fellow who proclaimed his enthusiasm in a voice of authority. He said: "You see, you've got to paint with pure cobalts, pure vermilions, pure veronese, I still think Derain was a bit afraid of him but he admired him for his enthusiasm and his passion."'

This initial meeting paved the way for the visit—almost a state visit—which Matisse paid to the two men at Chatou and, as he reported:

'The painting of Derain and Vlaminck did not surprise me, for it was very close to the studies I myself was doing. But I was moved to see that these very young men had certain convictions similar to my own.'

Matisse had expressed these convictions in pictures like the *Sideboard and Table* (Private collection, Washington), painted early in 1899, or in the studies of Bevilacqua, the nude model. These clearly establish that Vlaminck's claim to be the first Fauve can hardly be substantiated; and the dependence on pointillism, demonstrated by the former picture, indicated the source tapped by Matisse and Derain later in 1904, when they were elaborating the Fauvist approach properly so-called. Derain himself certainly considered that Matisse played a prominent, if not a vital, part in furthering this style, in the 1900–1901 period as is borne out by his own statement already quoted.

Unfortunately for Derain, his opportunities for putting into practice the lessons he had learnt from both men were strictly limited owing to the fact that he was called up for military service. After spending the summer at Belle-Isle in Brittany where Matisse had stayed the year before, he joined the 155th Infantry Regiment at Commercy. His period as a soldier obviously left him little time for his own pursuits; he managed to paint *The Ball at Suresnes* (Fig. 4), and a portrait or two, as well as to execute some decorations for the barrack walls (which were subsequently whitewashed over owing to their subversive character) and the illustrations for Vlaminck's two books, *D'un Lit à l'autre* (1902) and *Tout pour ça* (1903), published by Offenstadt. For the rest, he did little more than sketch out the plan for a novel, compose a poem—and write to his friends, above all to Vlaminck.

His epistolary exchange with Vlaminck is of fundamental importance for an understanding of his art and character; for instance, it makes clear that the impression sometimes given of Derain's early days in Paris and Chatou, not least by Vlaminck, that he was almost completely under his tutelage, is largely erroneous. Naturally he was eager and willing to learn from such a powerful personality; however, his words also reveal that as a man, endowed with a sharp intelligence, his own opinions were decided. His letters, direct and frank, not only provide some account of the dreary round of barrack room life and of a *simple soldat's* pleasures—visits to cafés and brothels—but give a spirited and intriguing insight into his intellectual processes.

After the companionship of Chatou and Paris, Derain's need to exist on his own resources compelled him to take stock and to work out his own position and this was increasingly at variance with that held by Vlaminck. It was a point of view, ably put in all conscience, that was nourished by his reading; and Zola, Balzac, Paul Adam and Nietzsche were amongst the authors he studied at the time. Contact with the realities of military life, moreover, turned him against some of the ideas he had hitherto espoused; thus, in what would appear to be one of the first of the letters sent to Vlaminck, he abandoned the anarchical ideals current amongst his friends:

> 'I will return feeling very old and bitter and even more sceptical than before—sceptical about anarchism, socialism and philanthropy.'

This apostasy is understandable enough and may be partially explained by circumstances: the transition from the free and easy life, Bohemian and certainly enjoyable, that he had led as a student, to the discipline and discomfort of the barracks.

Youth is often a victim of doubt and some of the opinions advanced by Derain may be considered as no more than a reflection of his growing pains; all the same, his constant questioning of values reappeared in later years. He was a born sceptic. There is, in fact, a pen-portrait of him, as he appeared to Vlaminck at this period, which, though written many years later, is worth quoting for it stresses the way he struck his closest friend—as a doubter and a seeker. Here are his words:

> 'Derain was blessed with a highly developed critical sense and a very personal way of seeing people and things. His was the ability to examine matters very deeply and to resolve the most difficult questions as well as the simplest problems, but the conclusions which he reached and his philosophical and artistic controversies often made him doubt himself. When he gave an ambiguous reply, a note of mockery would appear in his eyes, while the little pout of indifference playing on his lips would denote his ease in the world of ideas and reflect his inward laughter.'

Vlaminck's observations are confirmed by the temper of the correspondence. In fact, Derain was the prey to two main preoccupations: firstly, his realisation of his own lack of certainty as to ideas, aims and institutions and secondly, his need to work out some means by which these perplexities could be countered and resolved. In writing of naturalistic ideals, for instance, he declared:

'Such doctrines have above all taught us to belong to our own period. However, seized by doubt as I am, I propose to attempt something most difficult: to belong to all time. By doing so, it will lead us towards truth and simplicity and that, if one wishes to adhere to one's own era, is still more complicated.'

Again, in another letter, he wrote:

'Doubt is everywhere and lies in everything.'

His consciousness of the difficulty of discovering a firm route amidst the complex and contradictory ideas of *fin de siècle* France is clear. Nevertheless, in a closely reasoned letter of 1901 in which, amongst other matters, he discussed Nietzsche's conception of values (a term taken over, he maintained, from painting), he stated that it was 'the diversity of forms which reveals the power of unity', going on to argue, in a passage of some cogency, which is not without some bearing on his general standpoint, that:

'The man who loves form simply for its own sake is limited and lost. One must remember that such a man has a fashion, and a span of time. But the man who seeks the eternal elements in form can grow eternal himself. Thus, I don't believe that we ought to fear the diversity of our sensations. If we are not endowed with the power to bend them to our will, so as to extract unity from them, we are impotent from the start. And if this is the case, we have no hope of becoming powerful: it means that we lack a necessary value, that is all.'

Two years later in a letter of 1903, while telling Vlaminck 'I don't doubt so many things as formerly,' he returned to elaborate this concept of unity:

'One ought to try and establish the same relationship with the complicated matters of the human heart as with nature . . . I remain a realist, in the sense that, objectively, I do consider that no difference exists between a tree which is created, lives and dies, and man and that, equally, the thoughts and despairs of man, ought to undergo a parallel development to the tremulous movement of a leaf: their existence is solely conditioned by their environment. And that is unity.'

Derain did not seek to cast his ideas into any consecutive and ordered form. Nevertheless, he was evidently tempted by speculations which, in a more deliberate manner, were expressed by various contemporary writers; and his feeling for determinism, for unity and pantheism—for the inner spirit which motivates and stirs men and movements—does bear some relationship to the theory of *Unanimisme*, as propounded by Romains and Vildrac, which crystallised at this time. Broadly speaking, these writers sought to substitute a study of the collective soul, and of the consciousness of the group, for that of the particular individual, and in this aim they were influenced by the sociological ideas of the day. It is doubtful if any direct and formal connection existed, at this or any other stage, between Derain and these writers (although his friend Max Jacob was later in touch with Romains) but they did share conceptions that were dependent upon the age itself. Yet, as Tristan Tzara pointed out, neither the Fauves nor the Unanimistes

'were capable of deeply appreciating the movement of ideas that heralded the forth-coming disturbances of war and the social transformations that followed. Such historical currents found an echo in their sensibility. They were, in fact, the half blind instruments of the chief forces of their period.'

Derain's own recognition of the need for the existence of a new style in paint-ing was brought out in his letters; and in one of his earliest communications with Vlaminck, he declared:

'I am aware that the realist period in painting is over. We are about to embark on a new phase. Without partaking of the abstraction apparent in Van Gogh's canvases, abstraction which I don't dispute, I believe that lines and colours are intimately related and enjoy a parallel existence from the very start, and allow us to embark on a great independent and unbounded existence . . . . Thus we may find a field, not novel, but more real, and, above all, simpler in its synthesis.'

Clearly, both Van Gogh and Cézanne—the former in his view was more 'theoretical' than the latter—meant much to him and in 1902 he informed his friend that Van Gogh's

'memory haunts me continuously. More and more, I see the true meaning of things and it seems to be that our objective ought to be the fresco. Take Michelangelo, for instance: as sculpture, his overpowering nudes, aimless in a sense, don't they seem to you to be stupid and isolated?

In such comments, now as indeed later on, Derain revealed the sharpness of his observation and the complexity of his mind; thus, in discussing Cézanne and Lautrec, he said:

'I feel that their work was too perfect and thus perhaps too egoistical, and those natures that admire them do so because their own ambitions are reflected in them. Is this the true road to follow? In one sense, intrinsically, yes; but from a universal point of view, no.'

During these years, Derain was trying out ideas, discussing and discarding them as he went along, and his conceptions were to alter and evolve with the years. In perusing his letters (in the light of what was to occur later on) it is perhaps permissible to suspect that he was already engaged by a conflict which ever seized him—between the desire to obtain a grasp of the immediate and the instinctive and an equally firm determination to render the tangibility of the visible world:

One ought not to forget that the only complete definition of art lies in the transition from the subjective to the objective.'

In keeping with such ideas, and a consequence of them in fact, was his wish to study children's drawings ('doubtless truth lies in them') and he argued that:

'The great mistake of all painters, I believe, is that they have sought to render the effect of a moment in nature. They have not grasped that this effect proceeds from causes which do not arise from the ordered sequence of our impressions in terms of painting: they have not realised that a simple grouping of light can give one the same experience as an actual landscape. In short, isn't that what we ought to aim at?'

Despite Derain's belief that the moment was propitious for a renewal of artistic forces and for the adoption of a fresh and different style, he was unable, either at this time or at any other, to overlook what he felt was due to tradition and to suppress in his own mind the relevance and lessons of the past. This solicitude for his heritage transpires in his statement:

'Our race enjoys a quality which may develop into a defect: the cultivation of principle and our limitation by it. However odd it may sound, one ought to aim at being Corot while having undergone an apprenticeship under Poussin. Delacroix especially deserves attention and understanding; he has opened the door to our era.'

These were prophetic words.

The principal picture he painted during his military service, *The Ball at Suresnes*, 1903 (Fig. 4) with its echoes of Vallotton and Suzanne Valadon represented soldiers off duty in a dance hall and recalled the social comment of Vlaminck and his set or the writings of Charles Louis-Philippe. The virile reds and blues have a tang reminiscent of a rough local wine, and the powerful, if somewhat wooden, handling, leads on to the strong and rather cluttered *Still Life* of 1904 (Fig. 7) where Derain's debt to Gauguin and to Cézanne is evident, and, at some remove, to Bonvin and Ribot, not that his colouring was as sombre as that of these two men. The analogous treatment of forms and colour in *The Bedroom* (Fig. 6) or the *Boat on the River* (Mr. and Mrs. Lazarus Phillips, Montreal) may indicate that these date from this period rather than from the years 1905-1906 to which they have usually been assigned.

The problem of working out the chronology of Derain's work is ever difficult owing to his ability to ring the changes on different styles at the same time—and this delight in moving from one manner to another is already evident in the small *Still Life* (Private collection, Lausanne), which is treated in a more simplified and even abstract fashion than Madame Baron's *Still Life* (Fig. 7), painted in the same year. But the delicacy of handling shown in the smaller work indicated that he had achieved that limpid and enchanting feeling for liquid paint, so characteristic of his early years. That he should have succumbed to the attractions of pure colour was due not only to the general trend, but also, as he himself acknowledged in later years, to his pleasure in being a free man again after service in the army: his enjoyment of colour was symbolical of his new-found and much appreciated liberty. Moreover, through the intervention of Matisse, who together with Madame Matisse had called on his parents before he undertook his military service, he was now at liberty to become a professional painter. Against Vlaminck's advice, he even spent some time working at the Académie Julian.

By now he had found his own way, and the extent of his development was revealed in *The Bridge at Le Pecq* (Fig. 9) of 1904. In this fresh and effective canvas, the sketchy treatment, the elongation of the hands and arms (which may owe something to Marquet), the high colour and the use of black to outline trees, stress his independence, and its stylistic character indicates that *Barges at Chatou* (M. Roger Gros, Paris) or the *Snowscape at Chatou* (Fig. 8) belong to the same phase. In the latter picture, which recalls Pissarro's Norwood canvases, Derain characteristically evokes a mood of loneliness, and his placing of the central figure in a landscape anticipated *The Road at Camiers* (Fig. 28) of 1911.

Although he tackled themes that also tempted Vlaminck—not that he was ever so subjugated to this artist as is often claimed—the pointillist technique of *The Bridge at Le Pecq* (Fig. 9) suggests that he had also drawn closer to Matisse who was himself deeply involved in this style. The attraction of Neo-Impressionism was understandable enough, and the younger generation had the opportunity of seeing prime examples of such painting at the Signac exhibition held at the Galerie Druet in December 1904 or at the Cross exhibition at the same gallery of March 1905 or at the Seurat *rétrospective* at the Salon d'Automne of this year.

Derain's debt to Matisse was considerable at this stage and, through him, he was introduced to Ambroise Vollard, in whose shop he was privileged to see many important 19th-century French paintings. In February 1905, moreover, Vollard offered him material aid by purchasing the entire contents of his studio, with the exception, curiously enough, of the copy after 'Ghirlandajo's' *Christ carrying the Cross* (Kunstmuseum, Berne) which the artist wished to retain for himself. Derain and his older friend were clearly on warm terms; Madame Matisse, so Miss Alice Toklas recalls, was especially drawn towards him, and she exhibited in the Salon des Indépendants of 1905 a tapestry woven from one of his designs. Matisse's own role was primarily avuncular and he encouraged Derain to send four pictures to the same Salon, each of which was sold for 50 frs apiece. Such was the closeness of their relationship—one stressed in the brilliant portraits they painted of each other that are now in the Tate Gallery—that in the spring of that year, Derain joined the Matisses, who were installed in the charming village of Collioure on the west coast of France.

They were together then at the crucial moment when Fauvism flowered and when Matisse, having digested the lessons learnt from Cross and Signac,

14

achieved the lyrical, translucent and winning style so typically represented by the *Landscape at Collioure* (Statens Museum, Copenhagen) and the *Open Window* (Mr. and Mrs. John Hay Whitney, New York). He went all out for colour—gay, light and decorative—and this was used to translate his sensations into vibrant canvases and to evoke the '*Bonheur de vivre*' celebrated in his impressive canvas of 1906. Derain required small incitement to participate in this appreciation of the sunshine and light which made the coast so enchanting. In *The View of Collioure* (Mr. and Mrs. Charles Zadok, Milwaukee), *Collioure Mountains* (Mr. and Mrs. John Hay Whitney, New York) and *Collioure* (Fig. 11) all is delight; reds, blues, pinks were used to edge in the roof tops or to outline a horse and cart; oblong strokes, dabs with the brush, placed on the canvas rapidly and spontaneously, render the trees and foliage, in a manner reminiscent of Cross and Van Gogh. Yet what ought not to be overlooked is that such pictures formed a logical continuation to an approach already in evidence with the Chatou series. The elements were previously there; and his proximity to Matisse at this juncture did not so much radically change his manner as assist his employment of a heightened colour.

However, a different note was sounded in *The Golden Age* (Fig. 14), which, according to M. Leymarie, was painted at Collioure during the summer. The technique of this unusual picture may have been prompted by Matisse's extremely divisionist *Luxe, Calme et Volupté* (Private collection, Paris), executed at St. Tropez during the winter 1904-1905 and exhibited at the Salon des Indépendants in the spring, where it was promptly acquired by Signac. Whereas Matisse had selected his subject from a relatively modern poet, Baudelaire, Derain turned to classical antiquity, to Ovid's *Metamorphoses*—that vast treasure house of iconology that had appealed to Raphael, Titian and Rubens as well as to many others, and, in doing so, he reverted to a tradition which, quite recently in France, had been followed by Bonnard, Maurice Denis and K. X. Roussel. Nor was he alone; and in this year, Jean Puy painted his *L'Après-Midi d'un Faune*; Matisse was working on the *Bonheur de Vivre* (Barnes collection, Philadelphia), at the same time as Derain executed *The Golden Age*, while in 1908 Friesz painted *The Golden Age* in the Petit Palais, Paris. Derain did not attempt to present a calm Arcadian scene (as did Matisse); rather he endows his composition—so markedly divisionist—with a touch of what might be termed 'expressionistic' neurosis, and this characteristic stresses the connections—loose rather than precise—between the French school and the then modern movement in Germany.

The relationship between the visual arts and literature at this stage—those vital years just before the first world war—has not yet been fully examined, but Derain's letters to Vlaminck, as well as his constant interest in books, underlined his own keen concern for intellectual problems. Such comparisons, if they may be made at all, are generally little more than fortuitous, pointing

15

to certain correspondences in feeling and in subject matter. Yet, as Mr. Benedict Nicolson has observed, some parallelism existed between Matisse and Gide in the 1900's; both men can be observed, he remarks, emerging out of the gloom that enveloped the turn of the century:

'Into the blazing sunlight, the lush and faintly morbid gaiety, in the one case of *Luxe, Calme et Volupté* and in the other of *Les Nourritures Terrestres*'.

The quest for intellectual freedom (in Gide's case, for liberty in the widest sense) was shared by both artists and by many of their contemporaries; and in this search—a reflection of which, at a more elevated level, may be found in Bergsonism—'rules', as Matisse remarked, 'have no existence outside individuals.'

All was staked on the individual's rights, his feelings, his sensations. And it was the intuitive, as opposed to the perceptual, conception of art, that directed Matisse's own painting and, at this stage, Derain's as well. A comparison between the ideas adumbrated in Derain's letters and those outlined in Matisse's credo published in *La Grande Revue* (December 1908) establishes the points of similarity between them and shows how independently both men had adopted certain positions with common affiliations; indeed, the fact that Derain's views on unity, on intuition, on 'primitivism', had been sketched out when his relations with Matisse were little more than perfunctory, when they were no more than acquaintances at the Académie Carrière, emphasises that he was by no means dependent on his senior colleague. It is equally significant that he was already prepared to differ from Matisse. In formulating his views on light and colour, to Vlaminck on the 28 July 1905 he declared that:

1. 'A new conception of light consisting in this; the negation of shadows. Light here is very strong, shadows very faint. Every shadow is a whole world of clarity and luminosity which contrasts with sunlight: what is known as reflections.

Both of us, so far, have overlooked this, and in the future, where composition is concerned, it will make for a renewal of expression.

2. Noted, when working with Matisse, that I must eradicate everything involved by the division of tones. He goes on, but I've had my fill of it completely and hardly ever use it now. It's logical enough in a luminous, harmonious picture. But it only injures things which owe their expression to deliberate disharmonies.

It is, in fact, a world which carries the seeds of its own destruction when pushed to the limit. I am quickly going to return to the sort of painting I sent in to the Indépendants which, after all, is the most logical from my viewpoint and agrees perfectly with my means of expression.'

The fundamental lack of cohesion within Fauvism is stressed by Derain's statement; also, that even at the moment when two of its main protagonists were in close sympathy, divergencies of view on fundamentals were possible. His refusal to follow Matisse further than he himself wished to go did not prevent him from forming one of the group—Matisse, Manguin, Friesz, Vlaminck—who exhibited at the Salon d'Automne soon after his return from

Collioure. On this occasion he was represented by no less than nine works, amongst them *The Drying of Sails* (The Hermitage, Leningrad) and two views of Collioure. This show made the public aware of the existence of a band of painters with radical aims, and Louis Vauxcelles, who dubbed them 'Les Fauves', declared that:

> 'M. Derain gives one a scare. I believe him to be a poster artist rather than a painter. The parti pris of his virulent imagery, the easy juxtaposition of his complementary colours will seem to some no more than puerile. His paintings of ships, however, would do well as decorations for a nursery.'

Derain's independence and his increased stature are more evident from the pictures painted in London in 1905 and 1906 which are amongst the most personal canvases of his Fauve period. The precise date of his first visit to London has given rise to some confusion and it is sometimes maintained that this occurred only in 1906; however, both the artist himself and Madame Derain have confirmed that he crossed the Channel in 1905, and owing to his engagements at Collioure and Marseilles in the spring and summer, this journey presumably took place in the autumn. The identity of the pictures painted during his first stay is not known for certain, but it is generally assumed that the two pictures representing the Houses of Parliament (in the Musée de l'Annonciade, St. Tropez, and in the Pierre Lévy collection, Troyes, Fig. 12) date from 1905, and in view of their distinctive handling it might be safe to assign these works, as well as the *Reflections on the Water* (Musée de l'Annonciade, St. Tropez) to the latter part of that year. What is also unknown is whether or not they belong to the series of London views commissioned by Vollard as a sort of sequel to Monet's Thames views which were so successful when shown at his gallery in May and June 1904. Derain himself spoke of a group of nine pictures that he had executed for Vollard in the spring of 1906, and this set definitely includes *The Pool of London* in the Tate Gallery. As there is every reason to suppose that Vollard was the only dealer who provided him with such an opportunity, it is just possible that the first London pictures (if rightly assigned to 1905) were painted independently.

The establishment of such minutiae of chronology is of some importance for an appreciation of the twists and turns of Derain's art at this date. There is a difference in style between the two views of the Houses of Parliament which are couched in the Neo-Impressionist idiom and clearly owe a debt to Matisse and Signac and the later London views. In *The Pool of London* (Tate Gallery, London), the *Blackfriars* (Glasgow City Art Museum and Art Gallery), the *Barges on the Thames* (Temple Newsam House, Leeds), and *The House of Parliament* (Mr. Robert Lehman, New York)—the touch has lightened and the pictorial effects are more deliberately decorative, with twirls and lighthearted passages of paint. The almost watercolour effects of the sky, and the use of colour to build up the composition in terms of the surface rather than in depth, and the carefully disposed rhythms recall the Chatou pictures of 1904; in other words, the second London group may be seen, more or less, as an implementation of the words written to Vlaminck from Collioure; that he wished to return to the style of the Indépendants. Not that he intended to go in for a realistic manner, and as he told Vlaminck:

> 'It's absolutely essential to get out of the circle in which the Realists have shut us in... Thus it is understood that the relationships of volumes can express a light or the coincidence of light with this or that form.'

London, he avowed many years later, held an undeniable charm for Derain; he spent many delightful hours there wandering about, popping into pubs and frequenting the music halls, which evidently appealed to him. As ever, he passed a good deal of time in galleries and museums, devoting particular attention to primitive and African art. And like so many French painters, he closely examined Turner:

> 'Turner's work justifies Manet and the later men, and has in it something different as well—Humanism.'

His affection for London transpires too from the enchanting visions of Regent Street (Gelman Collection, Mexico City), and Hyde Park (Fig. 13) with their Nabiesque figures, art nouveau flourishes and Gauguinesque pinks. There, as Georges Duthuit charmingly wrote:

> 'with impeccable coolness, this well-bred lion lifts his hat to the Ophelia of Hyde Park, walking her spaniel along a path lined with currant bushes. Very smart, the varnished rocking horses and the compatriots of Constable, as still as though getting ready for a game of whist, strolling about on their backs in imperturbable violation of the laws of perspective: another difficulty which the painter, nonchalantly, counts as nought. Vermouth sward, azure trees—and enthusiastically he enumerates the charms of a pink and green jewel.'

Derain's need for change, and his essential restlessness renders it exceedingly difficult to chart the course of his evolution during this revolutionary period; so much was happening, so much intrigued him. The task of tracing his steps is further complicated by the absence of concrete information on many important points. It seems fairly certain, however, that he visited L'Estaque, not in 1905, as is frequently said, but in 1906—a contention which is corroborated to some extent by his submissions to the Salon des Indépendants and the Salon d'Automne; for whereas no picture of this site was shown at the former in 1906, four were sent to the latter: that is to say, at the end of the summer. It was while there, presumably in the summer of 1906, that he wrote to Vlaminck:

18

'To sum up, I see myself in the future painting compositions, because when I work from nature, I am the slave of such stupid things that my emotions are on the rebound ... To make things visual, that is to say, to amuse oneself by painting after the fashion of Denis, is to do no more than to transpose a theatrical decor. I believe that the problem to be faced is rather that of grouping forms in light and then harmonising them, while, at the same time, representing the matter available.'

In other words, Derain seems to have concluded that the translation of his visual sensations into their colour equivalents, equivalents which then assumed a pattern of their own volition, was not quite enough; he was determined to compose in terms of forms as well as colours, yet this establishment of a formal as well as colouristic harmony was achieved, none the less, almost exclusively by flat passages of pure colour. Already in the summer of 1905, as M. Leymarie points out, Derain, together with Matisse, through the agency of Maillol, who lived at Banyuls, very close to Collioure, had seen the collection of Tahitian canvases by Gauguin stored in the home of Daniel de Montfreid. Gauguin's influence was apparent in some of the London pictures but it was quite obvious in the *Turning Road, L'Estaque* (Fig. 16) or in the *Three Trees, L'Estaque* (Mr. and Mrs. Zacks, Toronto); the forms are more solidly anchored and the figures given a sharper outline than in the London series. The consequent simplification awards the picture a decidedly abstract appearance; the impression is given that it is deliberately composed rather than dashed off— as is the case with the earlier Fauvist canvases.

Once again, Derain, one suspects, was seized by the desire to discover a permanent artistic form, one that offered the possibilities of consistency and stability. It was characteristic, too, of his attitude at about this time, that he should have told Vlaminck, when writing of Monet:

'But, in fact, wasn't he right to render with his fugitive and durable colour, the natural impression which is no more than an impression, without lasting power, and did he not increase the character of his painting? As for myself, I am looking for something different—something which, on the contrary, is fixed, eternal and complex.'

Some understanding of the complexity and the strains and stresses of human nature may already be noticed in the few portraits from these years, mainly sketches, such as those of Vlaminck (Madame Kapferer, Paris), and the two heads of men—one of which is blocked in with Lautrec-like rapidity—in French private collections. His insight into character transpires particularly well in the head and shoulders of Henri Matisse (Tate Gallery, London) of 1905 in which he acutely underlines the 'professorial' aspect of his sitter or in the robust and quite unsentimental portrait of his father, Louis Derain (Messrs. Knoedler, New York) from 1906. As yet, surprisingly, given his later predilections, Derain revealed in his painting scant sympathy for femininity: he was barely tempted by the nude, although the character of his response to a painterly

19

model may be seen in the charming *The Dancer* (Fig. 5) in the Statens Museum, Copenhagen, evidently dating from 1906 and representing the same sitter as Vlaminck's *The Dancer of the 'Rat Mort'* (Fried Collection, Paris). The deformation and sharply rendered outlines noticeable in Derain's picture recall those found in *The Golden Age* (Fig. 14) and the unusual *The Dance* (Fig. 15) of about 1905-1906 which already conjures up his taste for the unusual and the esoteric, suggested by an amalgamation of Romanesque, Indian and Nabiesque influences. One wonders, too, if this work betrays an awareness of Bakst.

Derain's broad interest in the arts was already evident at this time. He was a discerning student, and it could be that the highly expressive contours used to outline the faces in the Fauve period were the consequence of his knowledge of Byzantine and Roman mosaics. It may well be so, for Derain at all times was keenly observant of earlier art, and later in the 1920's, his study of Roman and Pompeian mosaics and paintings bore fruit. A further sign of his curiosity was that his passion for a varied range of artistic experiences could be combined with decorating pottery (pp. 4, 159) which, at Vollard's instigation, was fired by André Metthey; these charming little *jeux d'esprit* anticipate the gaiety of his stage designs and underline his continuous interest in popular art.

Fauvism is one of those stylistic descriptions, purely accidental in their first application, that do not adequately describe a state of mind or a style of painting. True enough that, in a Vlaminck or a Van Dongen, a strain of the 'wild beast' might be found as far as subject matter or technique is concerned, but hardly so with Derain. During the short period in which he practised this highly coloured, instinctive and decorative style, he evolved an elegant, allusive, paradoxical, playful and sun-drenched language of colour; so much is clear from the Collioure and London scenes. He also sounded, only occasionally it is true, a note, at once more troubled and bizarre, but removed by very reason of its strangeness from the violent attacks of his old friend from the 'jungle' of Chatou. He was more refined, more perplexed, and the very deliberation of the method itself was too easy, too available, one might say, for a painter who found no advantage in 'a lack of culture'. If ever considering that 'the canvas remained a crucible in which to make living things', his apprehension of life itself and its intricacies and his realisation of the need to represent the unity of man and nature, inevitably turned him against a style which, when all is said and done, rendered, charmingly and sweetly, the *bonheur de vivre*—that is to say, as long as one was content to find arcadia in an appraisal of the surface alone. Derain himself remarked some years later that:

'Fauvism was our ordeal by fire.... It was the era of photography. This may have influenced us, and played a part in our reaction against anything resembling a snapshot of life. No matter how far we moved away from things, in order to observe them and transpose them at our leisure, it was never far enough. Colours became charges

20

of dynamite. They were expected to discharge light. It was a fine idea, in its freshness, that everything could be raised above the real. It was serious too. With our flat tones, we even preserved a concern for mass, giving for example to a spot of sand a heaviness it did not possess, in order to bring out the fluidity of the water, the lightness of the sky. . . . The great merit of this method was to free the picture from all imitative and conventional contact.'

'What was wrong in our attitude,' he went on, 'was a kind of fear of imitating life, which made us approach things from too far off and led us to hasty judgments. Where there is temperament, there can be no imitation. Thus it became necessary for us to return to more cautious attitudes, to lay in a store of resources from the outset, to secure patiently for each painting a long development.'

His dissatisfaction with Fauvism, also shared by some of his colleagues, notably Braque, did not appear at once, and certain canvases, datable to the period 1906-1907, like the *Landscape at Cassis* (Fig. 17) with its manifest debt to Van Gogh, or the impressive *Interior with Still Life* in the Bührle collection, Zurich, indicate that his interest in pure colour for its own sake was waning; nevertheless he was still to send some of his L'Estaque pictures to the Salon des Indépendants in 1907. All the same, a marked alteration in his style was to occur in the course of that year, a year in which he was called up for a short period of military service and in October of which he married Alice Princet, moving from Chatou to 'Les Fusains', 22 Rue Tourlaque, Montmartre.

During his Chatou days he had known many of the younger members of the Montmartre circle—Apollinaire amongst them, but from now on he came into closer contact with the group as a whole and signed a contract with D. H. Kahnweiler. He settled into this life with delight, especially enjoying the discussions that reigned over the café and restaurant tables: controversy appealed to him, and Gertrude Stein, who was not well disposed to him, records her disagreement with his views on the second part of Goethe's *Faust*. This side of his nature—that of a man who loved to speak his own mind—was also noted by Fernande Olivier in her acute account of him:

'Slim, elegant, with a lively colour and enamelled black hair. With an English chic, somewhat striking. Fancy waistcoats, ties in crude colours, red and green. Always a pipe in his mouth, phlegmatic, mocking, cold, an arguer.'

At this time Derain was pulled in a number of different directions, and, as an enthusiastic, energetic and intelligent young man—he was just twenty-seven —it was perhaps desirable that this should have been so. For instance, he responded to the enthusiasm for African art which touched many of the *avant-garde*, and not only in France; he bought from Vlaminck the African mask which still belongs to Madame Alice Derain, and his letters to his friend contain many references to such pieces as he was able to acquire. Notwithstanding his interest in African art, it would be wrong to assume that this materially affected his conception of painting; echoes of such work, as indeed of much else, constantly

21

occur in his art but their presence was due to his general inclination for 'primitivism'. A more potent influence was derived from Cézanne, thirty-three of whose pictures had been on view at the Salon d'Automne in 1904. The early *Still Life* (1904) in the collection of Madame Baron (Fig. 7) already suggests that he had learnt much from a master whom he later came to treat in an ambivalent manner but it was only in the post-Fauve phase that this artist demonstrably altered his style, and the return to a Cézannian manner may be observed in the *Interior with Still Life* (1906-1907) in the Bührle collection, Zurich.

His friendship with Picasso in the spring of 1907, when the latter was engaged in painting *Les Demoiselles d'Avignon* probably counted for much in his evolution. Derain evidently shared Picasso's desire to work on a large scale and in terms of the human form and *The Bathers* (Fig. 20) was painted in time for exhibition at the Salon des Indépendants—that is to say before the spring, when Picasso was starting *Les Demoiselles d'Avignon*. The general inspiration behind Derain's composition—more 'interesting' than successful, one must acknowledge—may well come from Cézanne's late *Bathers*, as indicated by the figure on the right hand side of the composition; on the other hand, the sharp accentuation noticeable in the body of the woman in the background carries some similarity with Picasso's work at this date. Her expressionistic features also suggest those found in African sculpture, and some echo of African art may likewise be discerned in a small study of *Three Bathers* (Herr Muller, Solothurn); however, in the *Nude Figures* (Fig. 19) the simplified decorative disposition of the figures is akin to that practised by Matisse in 1905-1906. He painted the nude again in *The Toilet* (Private Collection, Paris) but the figures are more 'classical' in feeling; the distortions are derived perhaps from Japanese prints. He certainly painted other figure pieces and, as D. H. Kahnweiler reported, he had:

> 'executed a whole group of pictures with life size figures. Some of these he exhibited at the Indépendants—thus a Bull, a picture with bathers. Fortunately the Bathers was sold and thus has survived. All the rest Derain burnt in 1908 . . . I saw these pictures for the last time in the autumn of 1907 at Derain's parents' house at Chatou. I particularly remember a large canvas with white and black women.'

One offspring of his interest, abortive at this stage, in the human figure was sculpture and the two stone figures, one upright, one crouching (belonging to Madame Alice Derain), are more directly moving than the few surviving pictures from this phase.

Unfortunately little is known of his feelings at this period. He was certainly dissatisfied by his venture into figure painting and by his attempt, however faltering, to experiment with a style of which the fundamental anti-humanism and savagery did not accord with his true nature. The Fauve landscapes make it clear, for instance, that he was at home with a sensuous view of life—an instinctive one—and that when it came to any intellectual distortions, he was apt to be gauche and uncertain; such efforts did not accord with his own spirit. One may suspect that his voluptuous, if often austere, delight in the body—in the pulsations of the blood behind the flesh, in the nooks and crannies of forbidden territory—was only able to blossom, as was the case later on, when his gaze was directed towards an ideal—that of the 'classical' nude, firm, unbending, almost heroic, or when he allowed himself, as occurred on other occasions, to be seduced by the charms, feline and all-embracing, of some delectable model.

To go outside a restricted range was not really his way at all. The point is that, though flirting with Cubism, as with much else, Derain never completely succumbed; wisely he realised that its principles in no way suited him; thus he avoided the fate of many of the Cubist epigoni. He was to draw back, turning with a sigh of relief, perhaps, to nature and to still life. One might interpret such a conventional little picture as the *Pots and Fruit* (formerly Galerie Kahnweiler, Paris) of 1908, unpretentious and humble as one of those arrangements of domestic utensils favoured by Chardin, as analogous to a sort of silent prayer offered up on arriving in a safe haven and as a sign of his delight at having found respite, if only temporarily, from more intellectual struggles in the contemplation of the quite ordinary matters of simple life. It was not that he wanted at all times to be so snug but he was unable to force the pace; his temperament would not let him be untrue to his own character; and he was sufficiently scrupulous to destroy, at any rate at this period, those works which he felt reluctant to defend.

His was the dilemma of an essentially severe artist who was compelled (how could it be otherwise at this particular juncture?) to reckon with new and rather overwhelming forces. That he was alive to the need for some form of discipline and prepared to take account of the trend towards simplification (already apparent in the more colourful Fauve years) transpired in the *Landscape at Cassis* (Fig. 18), presumably of 1907, in which a cut from nature was conceived in terms of blocks of flat patterns, which with their greens and browns constituted an equivalent to the scene itself. A similar degree of abstraction marked *The Hills* in the Rupf collection, Berne, with its heightened interest in the analysis of the surface, and it was this concern, allied to the use of ochres, light greens and browns, that brought him closer to Braque, so that a relationship, loose but evident, links his *Martigues* of 1908 (Private Collection, Paris) and the latter's *Road near L'Estaque* of the same year (Museum of Modern Art, New York); and in the summer of 1909 he was, in fact, to spend some time with this colleague at Carrières Saint Denis. But his own more characteristic approach appeared in the *Martigues* (formerly Galerie Kahnweiler, Paris) of 1908 in which the site permitted him to lead the eye back into the far distance, in accordance with the classical formulae.

23

Characteristically Derain was once again a prey to intellectual curiosity and Vlaminck reported that he was in the throes of experimenting with a model aeroplane and that his studio was filled with such objects. Then too he was conscious of the difficulties of finding his way forward and, as he told his friend in 1909:

'I don't feel the need to paint landscapes, portraits, still life. I've had staggering sensations of which the grandeur can only have its equivalent in an absolute possession of those forms which I can use as I please when I want to relive such moments; and it is most difficult to absolutely possess a landscape.'

One may even argue that his uncertainty as to which route to take, his very sensitivity to the atmosphere, to the limitations and problems of the time, was a sign of his self-awareness and of his refusal to be caught in an uncongenial mould.

He confessed to Vlaminck:

'Our uncertainty about the intellectual development of our age makes it difficult for us to desire a definite character. It is essential for us to submit to the unconscious. As for the result, we can only be the pupils of our own teaching, and to want to adopt an attitude is even absurd. One must follow life, happily, and derive the greatest possible pleasure from one's surroundings. When I say enjoyment I don't mean physical happiness; above all, I speak of the valuation of this enjoyment.'

His belief that the adoption of an attitude was 'ridiculous', to use his own word, may have led him to reject Cubism, and thus to part company at this point with friends like Braque and Picasso. This is not to say that he altogether escaped the Cubist influence—certain landscapes and still life pictures may be related to this style in terms of colouring as much as anything else—but he never went so far as to break the picture planes after the Cubist principle; all the same, a perceptive contemporary critic like Apollinaire, who had his finger on the pulse of the moment, could declare, and he was well aware that Derain was not a Cubist, that his liaison with Picasso 'had the almost immediate effect of giving birth to Cubism'. Derain, like Vlaminck, had realised that direct colourism was not sufficient; on the other hand, neither was prepared to completely surrender to the new style, and Cézanne offered a way out, one which they enthusiastically took.

Like his friends, he owed much to Cézanne. The series of impressive landscapes painted at Montreuil in 1909, like *The Red House* (Fig. 21) or the view at *Le Havre* (Private Collection, Paris) which has been assigned to this date, indicate that, for a short time, he adopted the refraction of light and the simplification of space, implicit in Cézanne's later works; further than that he would not venture; he declined to cut the link with nature itself. M. Bernard Dorival has admirably summed up the grounds for difference between Derain and the Cubists with his words:

'Cézanne's dictum about nature and the cone and the cylinder was susceptible of two interpretations; forms can yield the small cylinders and cones which are integral to them or the reflections and light which they engender; that was what the Cubists managed to do between 1908 and 1911. But by means of a contrary approach, one that is closer to tradition, one can lead the form towards the cylinder or the cone that is able to enclose it; that was Derain's method, and this permitted him to remain closer to figuration than either Braque or Picasso.'

In the well-known *Still Life* of 1910 (Fig. 26) the delicate tints of paint, sketched in as if in watercolour, the appraisal of the crockery and the angle of the table, suggest an appreciative yet personal valuation of Cézanne. A change had now occurred in his attitude: unlike the treatment of the *Still Life* in the Baron collection of 1904 (Fig. 7) or that in the Bührle collection of 1906-7, the touch is more translucent, the composition less cluttered. In a sense, too, his delight, a very puritan one, in such objects underlined his willingness to hoist his own flag; he was off on seas uncharted by the Cubists.

The difference between his intentions and those of these painters, forging ahead with their investigation of spatial relations, was shown in the series of firm and bold landscapes painted at Cagnes in 1910. The influence of Cézanne is still pervasive, notably in the *Cagnes* (Fig. 25) but in the picture of the same site (Gimpel Fils, London), one is not quite certain if the effect, again as if watercolour had been attempted, is deliberate or not. It is quite clear that Derain must have looked at Cézanne's watercolours and at his unfinished pictures like the views of Gardanne. But in others he was all out for solidity. In such works, he offered the result neither of his sensations in front of a scene, as rendered in terms of colour exclusively, nor of his appreciation of the pattern divulged by the dissolution of forms; he gave rather his observation, a little cold perhaps but telling all the same, of its solid, almost permanent elements, ones which, owing to its particular nature, and arising out of its configurations, allied itself to an appraisal of the 'cubic' values of appearances.

Slight alteration in a style, already outlined, occurred when he joined Picasso and Fernande at Cadaqués in the summer; all that was to happen—as the gaunt view of this town in the Basle Museum (Fig. 24) illustrates—is that his appreciation of blocks of buildings grew sharper; but neither at this stage, nor at any other, were his paintings as mechanistic as those of his more radical friend. He kept the contact with life. Abstaining from trifling with perspective, or dazzling and beguiling the eye by a fanfare of colour, he sought to affirm the very earthiness of the scene and to ensure himself that this was the very site he was painting. Figures appear only infrequently in such works, and when they do, as in the noble architectonic canvas *The Old Bridge at Cagnes*, 1910 (Fig. 22), they are invested with a hieratic calm; they are blended into the scene, forming part of the eternal order of life. In the midst of an era of far-reaching experiment, when all was subjected to analysis and questioning, when Derain himself, prime doubter, was constantly bedevilled by the complexities of his art, he came increasingly to look in a direction which led him, by slow stages perhaps but no less certainly, towards the maintenance of tradition (as he saw it), and towards a selective cultivation of the old masters.

He still continued to seek out the simplified ground plan of a composition—as in the *Road at Beauvais* of 1911 (Rupf Collection, Berne)—but the same year witnessed a demonstrable alteration in his style. What accounted for this, what made him relinquish the constructive phase, is not entirely clear; and it may well have been due to his chance encounter with a shepherd playing a bagpipe in the fields near Camiers, which is alleged to have occurred, and the sketches made there (it is said) were used as a basis for *The Bagpiper* (Fig. 32). Indeed, *The Road at Camiers* (Fig. 28), also painted there, certainly revealed a new softness and even sweetness. Yet if this picture represented an actual site, the *Bagpiper* was essentially a costume piece; or rather, it might be said, the placing of a sort of medieval survivor in the timeless landscape of the Pas de Calais emphasises the continuity of tradition, such as is found when the sophisticated traveller alights in some village where the festa in progress still preserves the allure and memory of ancient times. For the traveller it is a vision not quite disengaged from the baggage of his own experiences, so that the quaintness of the attire fuses with the souvenirs of what he has read or witnessed; thus, for Derain this figure, whether imaginary or actually encountered, is blended with his recollections of Renaissance Italian painting, with that perhaps of a Ghirlandajo.

The instinctive always tempted Derain, and this side of his nature was brought out in 1912 when he visited Vers in the Lot. Although he wrote copiously to Vlaminck, his letters often fail to be explicit on specific points of great interest and unfortunately he does not relate the reasons which prompted him to adopt a 'naif' approach in the landscapes painted there, and the one letter dealing with his stay is no more than enigmatic:

'Firstly, there are magnificent landscapes of two or three types but they are not all what you imagine. It's like those earlier ones, with a light which recalls that in the little Factory which you sold at the Indépendants.'

The pictures themselves are fascinating just because they stress the synthetic means Derain employed at certain periods of his life in order to express himself; and his utilisation of formulae from earlier masters permitted him, as in these works, to attain a style which, despite its echoes, was singularly fresh and winning. *The Church at Vers* (Fig. 29), for instance, incorporates his recollections of the Sienese and Florentine masters of the Renaissance or of those French artists who had been shown in Paris in 1904. The rounded hills and puffs of clouds are used for his own purposes: they seem to be integrated with his own visual attitude, and the same is true of the little clumps of trees and

26

the sweet Church; what is evident is a magical illusionism with more than a hint of the Douanier Rousseau. Yet what ought not to be forgotten is that we can see nature in the same way as did a Rousseau or an early Italian or French painter, that is, once our eyes have been opened.

Why did Derain seek in such pictures, as he evidently and consciously did, a means of returning to an earlier state of mind, and thus of showing the relevance of the 'primitive' (in the narrowest sense of the word) for the modern world? Was it an indication of the neo-traditionalism he was later to espouse? Or was it simply that he wished, conscious perhaps of his own sophistication, to present an instinctive interpretation of nature; a romantic gesture in an era of mechanisation? It may be significant of his point of view that he was discouraged after seeing Douanier Rousseau's *The Serpent Charmer* (Louvre, Paris) in the Salon des Indépendants of 1908. Did this constitute the true art? he asked Vlaminck:

'It seems hardly worth while searching and using technical training, when a person, so simple, so pure, such a dope in fact, can succeed in given such an impression; his work is the triumph of the dopes.'

In the light of Derain's view on the need for an instinctive form of painting, it is understandable that despite some initial reservations, he should have been impressed by Rousseau's art; one can hardly doubt that knowledge of his work turned him increasingly towards the search for a 'natural' style. This debt was primarily acknowledged in his landscapes; the *Valley at Morin*, 1911 (M. Pierre Lévy, Troyes), for instance, reveals a transitional attitude, in which the spirit of Cézanne is still acknowledged. It was above all in the Vers scenes that the connection with the Douanier was stressed, especially with the latter's landscapes of 1908. It could also be that the silhouetted stance of the '*Chevalier X*' (Fig. 43) was partly derived from Rousseau's portraits.

It is no less fascinating to discover that in the *Calvary* (Fig. 33) he adopted a religious theme, imparting to the dishes and coffee pot standing on the table an almost mystic significance, as if symbolically, he was referring to the Last Supper, the prelude to the Crucifixion itself. To this extent, therefore, the hint at a symbolical content, allied to the Italianate flavour of the composition, recalls the preoccupations of an artist like Maurice Denis. No movement, in fact, dies out without leaving behind some traces on its successors, and Derain's friend Max Jacob, for instance—whose *Les Œuvres burlesques et mystiques de Frère Matorel* he illustrated in that year—preserved in his gentle and whimsical work a strain of *fin de siècle* nostalgia and religious feeling. Nor ought it to be overlooked that an essentially modern spirit like Apollinaire was intrigued by medievalism, and that the *Enchanteur Pourrissant*, illustrated by Derain in 1909, had a medieval theme. Moreover Derain, lover of museums, student of literature, seeker after the esoteric, found much to intrigue him in the examination and evocation of the past—as did the supporters of a new literary classicism—a Moréas or a Charles Morice.

In the *View from the Window at Vers*, 1912 (Museum of Modern Art, New York), for instance, he not only planned the composition in such a way as to recall Renaissance Italian or Flemish painting, but reaffirmed his allegiance to still life, thus facing up to the problem that challenged him so often at this date, that of capturing the quality of simple objects spread out on a table; at the same time, with a typical *jeu d'esprit*, he arranged a complex interplay of double perspective. Still life was now to hold his attention and he underwent a short but intense period of experiment in this vein. For to Derain, the espousal of one style did not imply constancy on his part: 'it is no less true,' he had written in 1907, 'that the same personality can support two opposing theses without self-destruction.' Thus in 1912 and 1913, he painted a group of varied and brilliant compositions, ranging from *The Violin* (Private Collection, Paris) and the series of pictures with tobacco jars (which bear some relation to Braque's *The Match Holder* of 1911, in the R. Dutilleul collection, Paris, with their Cubist iconography and low colour gamme) to the magnificent Cézannian *Still Life* in the Chester Dale Collection, Washington D.C. or the more traditional *The Game-Bag* of 1913 (Fig. 37).

The variety of sources tapped by Derain in his still life pictures—the echoes of Renaissance Italy, of seventeenth-century Flanders and of a Manet or a Cézanne that may be noticed in them—might lead one to conclude that he was no more than a pasticheur, with little of his own to contribute. The point is that such researches permitted him to compose a series of pictures that win either by their ability to register the feel of shapes or conquer by their very fragility—those bowls, those pots of tobacco standing in such a lonely fashion on tables have the power to move us because, in their own silent, unoffending way, they emphasise the transitory character of existence. The one complements the other; in *The Game-Bag* (Fig. 37), he celebrates the spoils of an active life, and in *Still Life* (Fig. 27), he emphasises the introspective character that can be assumed by isolated forms. Besides the suggestive emotive aspect of such pictures there is the technical ability displayed—the result of his refined alert eye for colour, for subtle contrasts of greys, browns and greens, and of those gentle, caressing brush strokes which demonstrate his skill as a craftsman.

Derain's activity at this juncture was attested by his landscape paintings as well as by his still life pictures. In 1913, for instance, he painted a charming group of views at Martigues where Vlaminck and his family joined him for a week. In works like *Les Aloés* (Rupf collection, Berne) or the upright *View of Martigues* (Fig. 38) the familiar stylised puffs of clouds occur, but the effect is more akin to a tapestry: however, the softness of the blues and browns was strengthened by his introduction of stalwart oak trees that serve to hold the canvas in place. Such pictures were for the main, if not entirely, painted *sur place*—doubtless at that evening hour which so appealed to him. However, after his return to Paris in the autumn, he began to paint a number of forest scenes in the studio from memory, and these which probably include *Inside the Forest* (Fig. 30) and *The Trees* in the Soviet State Collection, possess a violent movement and an abstraction of forms curiously suggestive of Futurism and of Delaunay's interiors of cathedrals.

Just before 1914 Derain started to enlarge the scope of his art by returning to figure painting. He began to tackle the problems of expressing in the same canvas, mood, personality and formal values. In the study of a seated girl (Fig. 34) he employed for the first time that grey-washed 'Davidian' background which until the 1920's he used in order to isolate the figures and to conjure up the atmosphere which in his three pictures of this type was one of anxiety and tension. The faces are shaped as if carved out of wood, the hands are cut off at the knuckles; the bodies are placed uneasily in the chairs; and the space is made to press in on the figures.

The reasons that led him to embark on such works are unknown and once again no assistance can be derived from the correspondence with Vlaminck on this count. He may have wished to do little more than try out his hand in a manner that hitherto had failed to tempt him; but it does not seem as if his adoption of this style was prompted by any hint from Matisse or Picasso. They are certainly tinged with melancholy and evince a sympathy for isolation, as can be seen in the *The Two Sisters* (Fig. 39), the *Young Girl* (Fig. 34) belonging to Picasso, and *The Seated Woman* (*La Polonaise*) in the Barnes collection, Philadelphia. In *The Two Sisters*, (the models for which were Italian), Derain chose a muted colour scheme, placing the emphasis on the blocked-in outline, so as to render both weight and volume. In this picture and in its companion with their echoes of Trecento art, Derain succeeded in rendering, as no other artist of this time in France, the loneliness of these creatures, dumb and lost, and their acceptance of life. In doing so he may be considered as a precursor of that current of stark realism which has emerged in recent years. Such portraits, or rather studies of states of mind, reflect perhaps a touch of that interest in psychology of which the most radical exponent, working in a very different and more explosive style, was Oskar Kokoschka, himself an admirer of Derain.

Even when attempting a straight portrait of an identifiable sitter, like that of Madame Kahnweiler (Private collection, Paris), Derain chose to show her, not smiling and charming, but austere, even a trifle formidable. In this work, as in the *Self Portrait* once in Madame Paul Poiret's collection, he also confirmed his debt to the Italian Renaissance: Madame Kahnweiler is placed against a flowered background, and her head is modelled as if by a sixteenth-century Florentine (perhaps a Fra Bartolommeo) while his own portrait is inscribed on top of the canvas in a Renaissance manner. This taste for the past transpires, too, in his remarkable *Self Portrait* (Frontispiece) in which he depicts himself as if he were the donor in some early Flemish or French painting, with a stubborn wooden face—so different in fact from the aesthete encountered in another *Self Portrait* (facing p.8) from about the same period. Here, the concern for silhouette, immaculate and precise, is comparable to that of the '*Chevalier X*' (Fig. 43) in Leningrad—a conscious venture in naiveté, not perhaps without its influence on Modigliani and Giacometti.

Until the 1910's, with the exception of *The Golden Age* (Fig. 14), the *Turning Road, L'Estaque* (Fig. 16), and *The Bathers* (Fig. 20), Derain had not seriously tackled large-scale composition; his range was narrower and, on the whole, he was content to engage in a series of different yet absorbing essays in landscape and still life. Yet the situation changed radically on the eve of the war and already in the *Calvary* (Fig. 33) and *The Offering* (Fig. 36) with its African echoes, he had displayed a keener concern for subject matter and for more demanding themes. In selecting these he retained his old affection for still life. Thus in the highly important *Saturday* (Fig. 42), probably started as early as 1911, but finished only in 1914, there can be found the coffee pot, the open book, the plate with fruit on a napkin, the vase of flowers—all seen at that slight angle which he found so tantalising. Through the window may be glimpsed the customary Italianate sky—forming a contrast, perhaps, to the gaunt, self-absorbed, melancholy occupants, enclosed as if in a stage setting, who acknowledge their allegiance to African, Romanesque and Gothic art. These elements, different, even discordant, are fused together; we are made aware of their isolation; are these not the 'strangers', popularised by so many modern writers?

Their effectiveness becomes all the more telling owing to their simplicity which is stressed in the sharpness of the angles and the rigidity of the contours. And this simplification can serve to bring out the emotional content of a picture as in *The Last Supper* (Fig. 40); Christ is seen traditionally as the dominant and dominating figure: He and His apostles are depicted without their pupils being shown—a touch adding a monumental note to the picture. The table is bare except for the vase of flowers and a bowl; but the customary still life so favoured by the artist appears on a smaller table. Such static objects and Christ Himself act as foils to the restlessness of the other figures, blocked in and tormented.

May one see an attitude to life in these two pictures, *Saturday* (Fig. 42) and *The Last Supper* (Fig. 40)? In his instinctive intuitive way Derain may well have grasped that for the twentieth century, for the new world just around the corner, the loneliness, implicit in the latter picture, was to prove a compelling problem; that the very bourgeois existence suggested all the same by the unity contained in the scene was itself to be threatened. There is no evidence on these points, and yet one wonders if his preoccupation with the Cross in the *Calvary* and his choice of *The Last Supper* (Fig. 40) arose from a true concern with Christianity? Did his sharp intelligence, his sense for the inter-relationship between man and nature, his concern for stability, his feeling for the primitive and what was true, his growing realisation of the need for order, lead him to consider, if only for a short phase, that sacred art could still retain a meaning? Did this faith, if it existed at all, founder, like so much else, in the first world war? Or was he trying to get at the primitive emotions, thus choosing subjects like *The Last Supper* or the *Calvary* which he knew had been of deep significance to human beings in more primitive ages?

The elements that went to form Derain's style at this period were exceedingly complex and even contradictory. He was clearly receptive to all that was going on around him and eager to understand the past, looking not only at the Romanesque, Gothic, and Renaissance (as in his use of window frames)— but also, one suspects, at Indian and Byzantine art. He was probably acquainted with Byzantine miniatures and he was doubtless attracted by the simplicity and absence of detail to be found there—but he had no true understanding of the inner concept of the image, so fundamental to Byzantine art. It is this absence of a real grasp of the nature of Byzantine art which makes it meaningless to dub his painting from this period as 'Byzantine'. In this connection, however, it might be rewarding to come to some conclusion as to what was meant by 'Byzantine' at this time; however, to embark on an examination of this problem here would be out of place, but it is just worth remarking that for some theorists of the day—T.E.Hulme, for instance— Byzantine art appeared to have 'inhuman pessimistic' characteristics as opposed to the optimistic ones of classical and Renaissance art.

Despite such preoccupation, Derain continued to paint powerful still life pictures like *The Astrolabe* (Private collection, London); he had shown himself proficient with landscape and had investigated and finally rejected most of the modern art forms of the day. He had worked out, and of this there can be no question, his own manner. Since he had first evolved a personal style in about 1904, he had attempted to resolve the conflict between two elements—the instinctive quality of primitivism (seen as a means of renewing the sources of inspiration) and the constructivism, associated with Cézanne (considered as a means of representing the solid aspects of objects or of nature); these remained the principal forces that shaped his art, not only at this period but in the future. In effect, he endeavoured to hold the balance between extremes and to play the part, as André Salmon well put it, of a *régulateur*. The conflict between these two different strains in his nature allowed him to achieve a distinctive style, one capable of expressing his belief in the permanent inspiration of nature and also in the emotional potentialities of human life.

Derain's position in the modern French school was such that it was hardly surprising that Guillaume Apollinaire, in his preface for the exhibition held at

Paul Guillaume's gallery in October 1916, could write that:

> 'With an unequalled daring, he went beyond the most audacious forms of contemporary art in order to rediscover simplicity and freshness, the principles of art and the discipline which stem from such an exercise. After his early truculent essays, Derain has opted for sobriety and balance. From these efforts have emerged works, the grandeur of which sometimes take on a religious character and in which some have wanted to see (I know not why) traces of archaism.
>
> 'Derain's art is now marked with an expressive grandeur, which may only be termed antique. The works shown on this occasion reveal a daring and disciplined temperament. And a large part of his recent work retains a trace, moving indeed, of his efforts to conciliate two tendencies. He is on the verge of attaining his object—harmony impregnated with a realistic yet sublime beatitude. By encouraging daring while tempering it with temerity, one secures order. But that requires a considerable degree of disinterestedness. André Derain possesses just that quality.'

Derain was at Montfavet with Braque and Picasso when the war broke out and like the former he was called to the colours, seeing service with a motorised unit in Champagne, on the Somme, at Verdun, in the Aisne and in the Vosges. Thus he fully experienced all the sufferings of these tragic times; indeed four years in the ranks must have made their mark on him. As usual, he oscillated between two moods, writing in April 1915—much to Vlaminck's annoyance—of 'the delicious serenity aroused in me by the battle field.' However, by July 1917, after two more years of his war, and the terrible ordeals which France and her Army had endured, his tone had changed and he declared:

> 'Guns, guns, always guns. Mud, rain, dust—nothing to eat. Nowhere to sleep and always the same, always without respite. And the bombs, planes, night.'

In contrast to a writer who can turn to poetry or prose in such circumstances, a painter, unless commissioned as a war artist, has little opportunity of finding an outlet for his feelings, and except for an illustration in *L'Elan* (1915-1916), a few pastels and drawings, and some *repoussé* masks made from shell cases, Derain accomplished little at this time. However when on leave, he kept up with what was going on, reporting to Vlaminck in 1917:

> 'I have seen a great deal of painting which does not appeal to me at all. Its exponents are stuck in the mud and will have a lot of trouble to get out of it. But if the war is ever over, there will still be room for a tremendous shove. Cubism is really very stupid and increasingly revolts me.'

Yet his own work was by no means forgotten and in 1916 Paul Guillaume staged an exhibition of it in the Avenue de Villiers, Paris, the catalogue of which contained the famous preface by Apollinaire. He remained in the army until 1919, and a still life and a bouquet of flowers date from 1918, while he also undertook some sets for Claudel's *L'Annonce faite à Marie*, later performed by the Durec theatrical company in Scandinavia.

Shortly after his release from the army, Derain made his debut, properly speaking, in the theatrical and ballet world, when Diaghilev commissioned him to execute the sets, curtain and costumes for *La Boutique Fantasque* (music by Rossini, arranged and orchestrated by Respighi with choreography by Léonide Massine) which had its first performance at the Alhambra Theatre, London, on 5 June 1919. Fortunately, Mr. Cyril Beaumont, the well known authority on the Ballet, has left an impression of Derain on this occasion, one worth quoting:

'In appearance he was as little like the popular conception of an artist as it is possible to be. He was fair, clean-shaven, very tall and broad, with a massive chest and shoulders and large hands. In dress he affected a broad-brimmed felt hat set at a jaunty angle, soft collar, loose jacket, wide trousers and heavy brown boots. He had the most delightful unassuming manners and radiated the naive good humour of a child. He was very secretive in regard to his work. Whenever he was asked for details, he would reply *"A bientôt, vous verrez des choses merveilleuses."* But one night he offered to show his *projet* for the drop curtain. Very solemnly he withdrew from his waistcoat pocket a minute, folded piece of paper. He laid it on the table and slowly opened it, carefully pressing out each fold with the air of a conjurer engaged in a difficult feat of legerdemain. At last the paper was opened out and in the centre hardly more than an inch square, were a few lines covered with a wash of Venetian red. When he saw the black looks on the eager faces about him, he laughed with glee at the success of his little trick.'

On the opening night, Mr. Beaumont goes on:

'Derain was passing in review the dancers as they emerged from their dressing rooms. He was very particular on the subject of make-up and each artiste had placed on his or her table a tiny sketch showing what was required.'

Then the ballet began and after three metallic taps from the baton of the conductor:

'there commenced the lively, pizzicato notes of the *Marche Slave* which forms the overture. The heavy curtain swung up to reveal the drop curtain. The naïve treatment of the two figures posed against the broad masses of harmonious reds and browns recalled the decoration of an early Victorian pencil box. One received an impression of complete, all-satisfying joy.'

The success was instantaneous, so much so that when the collaborators stepped forward to take their call at the end of the ballet, Derain was frightened by the warmth of his welcome and had to be dragged on to the stage.

He was a born man of the theatre, gifted with the ability to render his designs lyrical and comprehensible, so that when translated into painted sets, they preserve an essential sketchiness. Such works, like his later sets, notably those for *Mam'zelle Angot*, contain no trace of the heaviness and seriousness sometimes found in many of his paintings. It was as if his need to transpose his sentiments into another medium acted as a liberating force, and his designs for *La Boutique Fantasque* (p. 35), spirited, witty, modern and utterly charming, accorded perfectly with the mood of the moment. His work, of course, had been shown in London before the war, in the Grafton Galleries' exhibition of 1910 and 1911, when Roger Fry had declared that the 'spirit of Poussin seems to revive' in it, but now, owing to the popularity of his ballet décor, he was to become the hero of the hour in English circles: and his influence may be discerned on Paul Nash and Mark Gertler.

In view of the taste for decorative painting existing in England at this time — as shown, for instance, in the various rooms painted by Duncan Grant and Vanessa Bell just before and after the first world war — the English appreciation of Derain was perfectly understandable. His ability as a decorator, so demonstrable in his ballet designs, was equally apparent in the group of little known paintings which he painted in January 1920 for the dining room of M. Walter Halvorsen, the Norwegian art dealer, at 6 Place du Palais Bourbon in Paris (pp. 52, 142). The set, which consists of seven upright and oblong canvases and four canvases with swags of fruit, demonstrates his skill in this branch of the arts. It celebrates the charms of femininity and his delight in fruit and flowers, and is radiated by an intense *joie de vivre*, emphasised by means of a rhythmical movement of line. The success of these decorations, which subsequently came into the possession of M. Georges Bernheim, inspires regret that Derain was not prevailed upon to paint others of a similar character.

Some idea of the esteem in which Derain's art was now held can be gathered from D. H. Kahnweiler, his dealer from 1907 to 1914 and from 1920 to 1922, who, in his *Der Weg zum Kubismus*, published in 1920, went so far as to say:

'In what respect Cézanne's great follower André Derain goes beyond him is easy to see; Derain also felt transformation of colour to be an evil. He strives to organise his structure in such a way that the painting, though strongly unified, nevertheless shows the greatest possible fidelity to nature, with every object being given its 'true' form and its 'true' colour ... there is no question here of the aesthetic worth of his austere and mighty art: he is one of the greatest of French painters. Cézanne and Derain will stand in art history, like the masters of the Trecento, as painters of transition, but in a reverse sense. Their solution of the conflict between representation and structure in painting will never result in complete success. Encouraged by their great example Cubism seeks new paths to the solution of this conflict.'

Although M. Kahnweiler's views were doubtless based on Derain's pre-1914 performance, his opinions, those of an alert judge of the modern French school, indicate the high hopes then placed on the artist. The severity of the later reaction against him, once his work was felt no longer to accord with the *avant-garde*, may thus be explained as the outcome of disillusionment. His stock, in fact, was high in the 1920's, and Mr. Clive Bell, subsequently one of

Four costume designs for *La Boutique Fantasque*.

his warmest friends in this country, sketched a charming portrait of him in his memoirs and provided a characteristically perceptive summary of his position in *Since Cézanne*.

'No one who ever met him but was impressed by the prodigious force of his character and his capacity for standing alone. At moments he reminds one oddly of Johnson. He, too, is a dictator, at once humorous and tragic like the mirific doctor, but, unlike him, infinitely subtle. He, too, is troubled, and not by any sense of isolation nor yet by the gnawings of vanity and small ambition. It is this problem that tortures him. Can he do what Raphael and Racine did? Can he create something that shall be uncompromising as art and at the same time humane?

'Face to face with that problem Derain stands for what is today most vital and valid in France—a passionate love of the great tradition, a longing for order and the will to win it, and that mysterious thing which the Athenians called σπουδαιότης and schoolmasters call "high seriousness". He accepts the age into which he has stumbled with all its nastiness, vulgarity and cheek.'

In insisting on what he termed Derain's 'high seriousness' Mr. Bell drew attention to that side of the artist's work which came increasingly to the fore in the immediate post-war period. This trend in Derain's art, understandable under the circumstances, may also be interpreted as a continuation and an amplification of the monumental style already attempted in his still life pictures and works like *The Last Supper* (Fig. 40) and *Saturday* (Fig. 42), the main difference being the adoption of a more direct and 'natural' manner. In his desire to secure a return to tradition (seen doubtless as a counter-balance to the anarchical and anti-artistic current represented by Dadaism, for instance), Derain was in step with some of the major men of his day; for at this date there arose a general call for a return to order; to this extent, therefore, he was exploring the same territory as several of his colleagues, not only in France but abroad, especially in Italy.

Towards the end of the war, he had confessed to Vlaminck that: 'I only want to paint portraits, real ones with hands, hair, life itself.' Soon after his demobilisation, his precepts were put into practice in the portrait of Paul Guillaume (Madame Walter, Paris), who was to succeed Kahnweiler as his dealer in 1922, and *The Greek Girl* (Dr. W. Raeber, Basle), both of which, painted in 1919, show a significant change in comparison with his immediate pre-war portraits. For while still employing the washed-in 'Davidian-like' background of neutral tints and the blocked-in figures, the forms themselves are softer, as if he had adopted some of Renoir's gentleness, and by so doing, he emphasised the human qualities of his sitters. A similar concern for the character of the sitter, rather than for the state of mind represented by a specific type, may be discerned in the portraits of Madame Derain (Private Collection, Paris) and Kisling (Private Collection, Paris), and increasingly he was to suit the style to the temperament of the individual.

The change that took place in his art may have been prompted by his visit to Rome in 1921. The quality of the work accomplished there, in any case, emphasises the inspiration he derived from his residence in the city and from his trips to the Campagna. Portraits like *The Italian Model* in the Walker Art Gallery, Liverpool (Fig. 47), probably painted in Paris after his return from Rome, indicate his eagerness to blend his new-found softness deriving from Corot and Renoir with monumentality; certain elements from the past, like the summary treatment of the hands, still persist, but the features are more rounded, more reflective indeed of life and gaiety. An altered mood was equally evident in his landscapes and he rejected an exclusively constructive treatment of the scene. In the *Villa d'Este* (Dr. W. Raeber, Basle), softly and felicitously, he evoked the tremulous atmosphere, flower-scented and harmonious, that reigns at certain seasons in Rome, and his response to the shimmer of the trees, the sense of mood that prevails there, recall the *sanguines* of Fragonard and Hubert Robert. Not that his sympathy for the angularities of a landscape was altogether abandoned, and in *The Road at Albano* (Fig. 48), the dryness of the terrain is matched by the sobriety of his colours, the firmness of the structure.

One may suspect that for Derain, as for a Poussin or a Gaspard Dughet, the contact with Rome, with all its eternal, evocative and dreamlike qualities, strengthened his determination to rely on tradition and made him realise, too, that this may be found in the present, its echoes and survivals at any rate. And this recognition was not only expressed in an ambition, discerning all the same, to understand the techniques and points of view of some of his predecessors, but in an awareness of the continuity in aims and moods that link a man to his heritage. The deep reservoir of subconscious memories that exist with all of us—the whole Jungian world of inherited spiritual and psychological baggage—may be carried in more ways than one; it can so operate upon the artist that he may only fulfil himself, and may only say what he wishes, too, if the past is used as a springboard. This was the case with Derain to an increasing degree; yet his affection for the past rendered it harder for him to attain the perfection he desired.

Derain's interest in classical art ought not to be taken to mean that he himself was necessarily or exclusively a classicist—or a neo-classicist in the sense of a Thorvaldsen or a Canova. To use such terms is often to invite disagreement; definitions shift from epoch to epoch and it might be more accurate to suggest that, at this stage, Derain was sympathetic towards certain earlier periods favouring those artists whose work appeared to him to constitute tradition. Like a Renaissance artist, he was prepared to take over motifs that appealed to him, either because of their relevance or else because they evoked a particular state of mind. In the 1920's, therefore, he was to look closely at Roman and Fayum portraits, at Roman and Pompeian mosaics and, in the case of

37

his designs for the ballet, *Fastes*, to employ straightforward classical themes. Yet he did not seek in the antique the historical antiquarian side; he considered that this source could provide an instinctive and brilliant answer to a specific problem. Thus, much later, in 1948, he maintained that:

> 'Intelligence. The ancients knew how to paint a glass of wine. They were really intelligent, understanding things deeply and not just with an intelligent glance—as Matisse does. Today everybody can be intelligent; it's too easy. So nobody any longer knows what it is, this gift, this direct way of seeing things.'

Many elements remained constant in Derain's art throughout his life; nevertheless his ideas underwent some change in the 1920's; thus the two interviews given to René Crevel and André Breton (who were, it must be remembered, Surrealists) in this decade, emphasise the evolution in his thought. He went so far as to readjust his views on Cézanne whom he had admired so much in the past, telling Crevel that:

> Cézanne bothers me. His desire for perfection is incompatible with the free play of thought. He seeks the absolute but this search is opposed to the expansion of life. The fallacy in every theory is the attempt to come across a definite solution. No system of moral thought lasts for ever and contains the possibility of constant renewal. The desire for the definitive—that's death.'

He was after the spontaneous, maintaining that

> 'The most beautiful works have their origin in *graffiti*. Art is a game, one which may prove sublime but which is still only a game. There is no possible initiation.'

And with an implicit reversal of his earlier views, he concluded:

> 'It's not the artist's role to educate the people; the people must educate him. It is the people who create words, give them their flesh, but the poet finds the rhythm. The greatest threat to art is too much culture. The true artist is an uncultivated man. The day when culture will become general, we will no longer need art. We will never find any consolation. But human things are not capable of perfection and, above all, the artist must decline to make a sorry spectacle of himself—as a man who is resigned to acceptance.'

Again, in his interview with André Breton, when he elaborated his ideas of spontaneity and lyricism, he made clear that he sought to pierce to the essence (as he viewed it) of a subject, arguing that:

> 'Here is a ball. In painting one has always considered it as a sphere and it has only been represented mathematically. However, it possesses more important properties—it can roll and when placed on a plane, it oscillates. It is elastic and can rebound. What would I have to say of the ball when I have made it round? It is not a question of reproducing an object but its virtue, in the ancient meaning of the word.'

Concluding this long and intriguing interview, which displayed all his verbal virtuosity and intricacy of mind, Derain, while confessing his admiration for the white point favoured by the Dutch seventeenth-century masters and for Corot and for Renoir, declared that an artist should:

'award to each object its proper place. The really lyrical man is a liar.'

Until the outbreak of the 1914 war, Derain's style had followed a series of clearly demarcated phases: these reflected his interest now in one problem, now in another. From the 1920's until his death, however, an attempt at tracing his stylistic evolution is less rewarding for an understanding of the development of his painting. Or, perhaps, one should say that he treated his themes according to the character of the subject or the mood of the moment, and, as he told Florent Fels, works of art are created for the milieu where they are conceived. The period of experimentation had surrendered, in fact, to one of consolidation in which he was less inclined than ever, except on rare occasions, to move outside a selected orbit.

During these years, highly successful ones, Derain practised several styles simultaneously; when he felt so inclined he would revert to an earlier manner for the solution of a particular task; his mind moved in different directions, embraced various and often opposing problems; and from the point of view of subject matter and importance each category, posing different problems and demanding different qualities, must be judged on its merits.

At the top of his form, Derain was after the Grand Manner. This search for a sort of 'history' painting, in terms of his own generation—already represented in several of his pre-1914 compositions (those descendants of the 'machines' of the Salon)—may explain the references made to him at this time as a Bolognese painter. Although no very evident connection, from the point of view of theme, colour, or formal language, links him with the seventeenth-century school, this interpretation of his work, advanced at a time when study of the period itself was still cursory, must have been based on the erroneous assumption that masters like Carracci were eclectics, in the sense that their art only presents lessons culled from the past, and not an individual contribution. Some connection, doubtless little more than fortuitous and surely not intentional on Derain's part, may be observed with the Carracci, especially Annibale, in so far as Derain, like the earlier master, was prepared to veer between a realistic and an idealistic manner if it suited his subject matter. Thus at the same time as he painted *The Kitchen Table* (Fig. 62), a naturalistic or realist composition *par excellence*, he was prepared to undertake a figure subject like *Pierrot and Harlequin* (Fig. 61) which, broadly speaking, could be classed as 'idealistic'.

In tackling this subject, apparently suggested to him by Paul Guillaume and based on an engraving from a scene from the Commedia dell'Arte, Derain went to some trouble to solve the compositional problems, executing a

39

drawing (Fig. 60) and an oil sketch (Lord Radcliffe, London). He took up a theme which had gained particular currency in the early years of the eighteenth century when Claude Gillot and Antoine Watteau had been intrigued by its evasive and poetical qualities and, at the hands of the latter, the unrealistic world of the comedians—hiding their sentiments and feigning others—had permitted the evocation of a world of pathos and unfulfilment. The iconography of the Commedia dell'Arte, to which Picasso had turned for his décors for *Parade* in 1919, evidently held a strong appeal for artists at this time; and Harlequin was painted not only by Picasso but by Gris; his figure, lonely, capable of romance yet often shunned by it, assumes for certain spirits a particularly elusive and tantalising character. Thus the typical components of Derain's style, like the jug, violin and bowl, and the undulating hills (reminiscent of Sanary, for instance), are subjugated to the two dancing figures; though no longer the woebegone sitters of *The Two Sisters* (Fig. 39), they are invested with the sad melancholy that repeatedly occurs in his pictures. They too have realised that acceptance may prove the only possible course of action; they stand uneasily, and Harlequin himself seems to reflect, half curiously, half whimsically, upon the emptiness of pleasure. In their inability to proceed, to gain more than there is to gain, one is reminded perhaps of the hopelessness that certain writers—a Beckett for one—have suggested in recent years. Thus Derain in this picture or in the *Harlequin* in the Chester Dale collection, Washington D.C. (Fig. 56), while taking a 'fancy' subject, was all the same able to make it reflect the spirit of the era.

The rigidity apparent in the composition is such as may offend modern taste, accustomed as this is to the linearism of a Matisse or a Picasso; this, in fact, is not surface painting but one in which the plasticity of the forms is sought after. Solidity had engaged Derain's attention ever since he had abandoned Fauvism, and many of the still lifes painted in the 1920's, notably *The Laden Table* (Fig. 53), and *The Kitchen Table* (Fig. 62) may be said to constitute a logical continuation of his researches, sombre as they often are, in contrast to such works as the *Still Life* of 1910 (Fig. 26). Once again, in the major compositions of this nature, one feels that Derain's aim was to sum up the results of certain researches into a comprehensive picture—a synthesis. His understanding of volumes, his solicitude for the disposition of forms, one in relation to the other, at this stage, relates him to painters like Zurbaran or Caravaggio. The connection with Caravaggism is apparent: the placing of the highlights along the edge of a table and the drapery in *The Laden Table* (Fig. 53), recall the Roman master's *St. Jerome Writing* in the Borghese Gallery, Rome which Derain could have seen when in Rome. By going back for his terms of reference, he presumably realised that he was placing his work in relation to the past, and was accordingly accepting the challenge of such competition, so that, in the last analysis, it is arguable that his willingness to face this test was a sign, not so much of a lack of confidence in his abilities, as of a belief in them.

This admirable host was prepared to offer a choice of wines; his still life pictures, for instance, can be judged dry or sweet. In the years when painting such taut works as *The Kitchen Table* (Fig. 62) he was equally prepared to adopt the gentle decorative manner of the *Roses* and *Still Life with Basket* in Madame Walter's collection or the *Vase of Roses* (Fig. 54), and in the latter the influence of Renoir may be detected. The roses are treated in such a way as to suggest the heaviness and softness of the blooms and their heady scent; yet also, in other pictures he could place a greater emphasis on the delineations of the petals and stalks as in the *Flowerpiece* (Fig. 52) with Dr. F. Nathan, Zurich, and in doing so remind us that he was the compatriot of Delacroix and Courbet. The contrast between these two different attitudes to still life, quite demonstrably intentional, which took place especially around 1924-1926, illustrates his perpetual oscillation between instinctivism and construction.

A not dissimilar development occurred when, true descendant of a Courbet or a Renoir, he became the enthusiastic recorder of femininity—choosing now the *gamine*, now the *femme du monde*, now the ordinary bourgeoise; models, pretty, alluring, dominating, *câline*, almost monstrous too—all are captured by his brush. He responded, happily, devotedly, to women—not forgetting the austere, so that M. Jean Leymarie's words that he was the 'Don Juan of painting', assume an appropriate significance. By its very nature, Don Juanisme stems from an infinite curiosity—and Derain was haunted by the desire to know exactly what each woman has to offer, in what respect she differs from another, and by a determination to plumb her own particular feminine quality. For any man who loves women (and not just one), the body itself becomes the object of a cult, in which certain special elements may count far more than others, and for such connoisseurs (given a degree of response), almost any feminine body perpetrates its appeal, its delirious and delicious incitement to a voyage of discovery. So it was with Derain in his painting. Thus, in *Nude with a Cat* (Fig. 57) of 1923, he renders all the proud architecture of the female form, so that the powerful legs and the firm articulated torso lead up to the softer, sensuous features. In *The Beautiful Model* (Fig. 55), voluptuous and iridescent, as if warm from the bath, the dreamy, gentle features are blended with her body and arms, which are themselves depicted with a caressing feathery gesture. Slowly and gently, the brush seems to stroke the canvas, as if the real body lay there to be awakened by the artist's touch. Pearly or nut brown, with their loose hair or tightly furled coiffure, with their firm, poised breasts, Derain's models (depending upon their nature) have a substance, an earthiness or a fey-like quality that is hardly rivalled in modern painting; and the range of his response also transpired from the set of prints entitled *Métamorphoses*. Such pictures with their determined expression of his cult of Venus

41

point to the continuity of a tradition that stretches back to the antique world.

During the 1920's, Derain tried his hand at many different subjects. Besides his nudes, still life and compositions like the *Pierrot and Harlequin* (Fig. 61), he painted various portraits—those of Vincent Muselli (Fig. 59) and Madame Guillaume (Mme Walter, Paris)—and a series of dancers (like those in the Art Institute, Chicago, and in the Phillips Gallery, Washington, D.C.) and male musicians, which display his customary technical skill. What is so fascinating about such pictures is that they show that he was quite prepared, in fact, to tackle subjects generally considered to be the appanage of the academic artist. Nevertheless his ability to succeed in such ventures is proved by the *Geneviève* (Fig. 66); his sure sense of design, for instance, came out in the *Harlequin* (Fig. 60). His diversity was also shown in the various ballet designs and book illustrations that date from this period.

He gave full measure of his gifts in the many landscapes dating from these years—pictures of Sanary, Les Lecques and elsewhere in the Midi that were painted on his almost annual visits to this region. In contrast to his Fauvist pictures, where colour had been keyed up to a pitch not discernible in nature, Derain now favoured a more restrained gamme—and his greys, blacks, browns, ochres and greens underlined the attention he devoted to his palette. He was still concerned to give the qualities of light but he now sought such effects in quieter places; he strove to capture the mysteries and secrets of Nature. In the intricately composed canvas of Ollioules (Fig. 51) of 1922 he endeavoured to render the structural growth of trees, their independence from vegetation, their inner life, one might say, but, in others—particularly in his Sanary landscapes—he was tempted by the undulations of hills and by their soft pulsating quality. He was now concerned with recessional values which he was anxious to establish so as to give the total effect of the scene; and he felt especially at home when able to provide a view of a panorama of trees and hills, or else of a winding road, sneaking like a snake through pines and olives.

Derain was at his most harmonious and brilliant in the series of landscapes executed at St. Maximin in 1930, in which his eye for tone, his sense of construction, and his grasp of perspective appeared at their best. Some idea of his compositional methods can be gained from a comparison of the drawing for the *Basilica of St. Maximin* with the finished painting (Figs. 68-69); here the forms established in the sketch are faithfully carried out in the finished canvas with the addition of particularly rich ochres, greens and browns. Such pictures clearly bore some relationship to his earlier views of Cagnes of 1910 (Fig. 25) in which his concentration on the treatment of a particular aspect of the scene—in this case the isolated formal structure of the buildings—awarded them a slightly artificial air, turned them into 'pictures'. Yet in these later works the individual character of the site and the style employed to render it are blended; what greets us is the view of a town, timeless, beaten by the sun.

42

In such paintings or in those executed previously in Rome, his debt to the early Corot is stressed; nevertheless when actually hung close to a picture by his predecessor, they do not fade away. They assume their own character, and in doing so, they demonstrate the validity of a tradition. In fact, a study of the development of painting—especially that of landscape—permits one to realise the continuity of vision that exists, linking one painter to another. And Derain's intuitive sense for nature, so well expressed in the *The Glade* (Fig. 71) with its mixture of greens, browns, and blues charged with high impasto, goes back to Courbet and Cézanne.

It is indicative of Derain's aims that, while painting his elaborate nudes or severe landscapes, he should have also tried out certain ideas in the form of sketches, and this particular manner of examining a project remained with him until the end. These small works—no more than essays for larger projects—are not inevitably satisfactory; all the same, they are most intriguing for the light they shed on the relationship between his artistic theories and his practice. They certainly show him in the throes of endeavouring to find a visual means of venting his views on spontaneity, and in this attempt, one may be reminded, especially in the small *Self Portrait with his Family* (Madame Alice Derain, Chambourcy), of his stylistic connections with sixteenth-century mannerism; the flickering highlights and elongated forms recall Schiavone or the early Tintoretto. The effects, in fact, are as if he was attempting to register the staccato effects of a conversation.

By the late 1920's, Derain was at the zenith of his reputation and, owing to the skilful enterprise of his dealer, Paul Guillaume, he enjoyed a considerable measure of prosperity; for instance, he was able to indulge his passion for fast motor cars. At this juncture, too, he was extremely sociable—as the memoirs of Clive Bell and Francis Carco attest, and he enjoyed café life and dining out, especially in the company of writers and artists. As Dunoyer de Segonzac has remarked:

'He was a faithful habitué of the Diner du Verre de Vin, founded by the Frères Peignot, Felix Boutreux and Bernard Naudin. He would find here friends like Charles Despiau, Pierre Roy, the sculptor Marque, the ceramist Lenoble, the painter Dignimont, the sculptor Pierre Poisson. And Derain, always very simple, joined with his friends in singing with much vivacity and feeling the old medieval songs.'

He had every reason to be content, at this period as he won the Carnegie Prize in 1928 for his *Still Life: Dead Game* (Fig. 63) and various exhibitions of his work were held in France, Germany, England and the United States. However, at the moment that success attended him and he had become esteemed as an international figure—his painting fetched high prices in England, for instance —a reaction occurred, and this was expressed in the volume *Pour ou Contre Derain* issued in 1931.

43

Although various painters and critics defended him in this publication, the case for the prosecution was put by Pierre Courthion and Jacques-Emile Blanche.

'What I dislike in his work,' said the first, 'what my eyes refuse to accept are his easy tricks that recall Besnard, and the complaisant way in which he will use his brush to round out an eyebrow or give it its contours while lifting his little finger.'

'The faith and brio which marked his earlier works', the latter declared, 'seem to have been replaced by the indifference of a sceptic weighed down by the number of masterpieces he has seen in museums and collections. His nudes and the series of heads still show intelligence and a painter's touch; poetry is still sometimes present, but it smells of fatigue. Youth has departed; what remains is a highly cerebral and rather mechanical art.'

Such pointed criticism did not curb Derain's activities at this period. He continued to be invited to execute ballet designs—notably those for *La Concurrence* with music by Georges Auric and choreography by Balanchine, first performed by the Ballets Russes de Monte Carlo in April 1932 and for *Fastes*, with music by Henri Sauguet and choreography by Balanchine first performed in June 1933—and to be shown in London and New York. Nevertheless he gradually began to retire from Parisian life, a tendency which increased once he had settled in his house at Chambourcy close to St. Germain-en-Laye, which was to remain his home until his death.

Exactly what occurred at this time is by no means easy to determine. It would seem as if a certain retrenchment took place, and this may have been due to the fact that he was no longer in his first youth; in 1935, for instance, he was already in his mid-fifties. He still preserved, however, his desire to paint in the grand manner, and his work ranged from curious and almost neurotic canvases like *The Two Men* (Private collection, Paris) of 1932, with its rather Lottoesque note of melancholy, to the rich and resonant *Two Nudes with Fruit* (Fig. 72), with its Venetian sonority and generous colour. His still life, too, showed no falling off in his ability to render the reflections and glitter of fruit. This same ability to invest a composition with glowing resonance is found in *The Surprise* (Fig. 73) of 1937-1938, where the female figures, with their allegiance to Renoir and Maillol, are harmoniously and invitingly displayed in the foreground; and the sense of opulent design, well shown in this picture, also marked *The Stag Hunt* (Fig. 74) formerly in the Art Institute, Chicago, from the same period. Such figures, of course, are not always immediately appealing and their very solidity, their woodenness even, can offend a generation largely reared on linearism and surface decoration. If certain nudes from this period—like *The Nude* (Madame Alice Derain, Chambourcy)—are not entirely successful, lacking a spontaneous sparkle, as it were, the vigour and force of his best pictures of this type awards them a special place in modern art.

Derain evidently faced difficulties towards the end of his life. It could be that he was increasingly preoccupied by the problems of incorporating into his art those aims and precepts dictated by his intelligence and wide knowledge of the past. His cult of earlier art and his respect for the Graeco-Christian tradition (in 1933, for instance, he disposed of much of his African sculpture and purchased Hellenic and Cypriot items in their stead) was clear enough, and they can be seen in the unusual *The Painter with his Family* (Fig. 75). The artist, surrounded by his family, gazes at the easel, unquiet and concentrated: just as with *Saturday* (Fig. 42) he has synthesised in this picture those elements that appealed to him at a particular stage—the open window derived from a Florentine painting, the serving girl who seems to step out of a Fayum portrait, the still life which might be encountered at Pompei or in an early Caravaggio, the parrot who could be met in a Snyders or the figure of Madame Derain, which is invested with the domesticity of a Dutch painting of the seventeenth century. This amalgamation of so many different strands seems surprisingly anachronistic for a twentieth-century painting, and yet Derain has managed to fuse them into a viable whole, one deriving part of its fascination from its revelation of his intentions and his state of mind at a specific phase.

The tradition of quotation in painting is a distinguished one, and such borrowings do not destroy the validity of the composition. In this connection, it is worth pointing out that the art historian will often fasten with delight on the evidence of such sources, demonstrating as it does the continuity of style, but, for the art critic, it often seems to imply only derivation—anathema in an age for which originality is of paramount importance. However, at the present time, critical opinion has begun to reckon with the possibility of the artist—a Blake or a Fuseli, for instance—adopting certain elements from the past, exaggerating them in their case, and yet painting pictures which are fascinating and intriguing. Derain's own connection with mannerism is complex in the extreme, and it would seem that his fundamentally classical outlook was also complemented by stylistic elements which might well be described as manneristic. The mood of pictures like *The Two Men* (Private collection, Paris), or *The Painter with his Family* (Fig. 75), not to speak of the smaller sketches (Fig. 87) and his use of *trompe l'oeil*, recall the artistic baggage of the mannerist artist. However, at the same time, he could seek out the solidity of objects, after the fashion of the seventeenth-century Dutch and Spanish painters, as is clear from the *Still Life* (Fig. 79) of 1939.

Towards the close of his life, Derain tended to concentrate on a narrower range. His interest in the nude continued, but only intermittently, and it can hardly be claimed that the figure pieces he painted rivalled the great series of the 1920's. It is possible that he did not wish to repeat himself in this direction and that his inventiveness, as far as a fresh approach was concerned, had tended to desert him—sign of his increasing age. On occasion, too, he painted portraits—those of Madame Lévy and her children (M. Pierre Lévy, Troyes), or of Madame Huri (Madame Huri, Lausanne)—and he could still capture the essence of a special mood, as in the moving head and shoulders of *The Deportee* (Fig. 77). He also responded to youth, painting a group of charming and affectionate studies of André, his son, in which a care for the child's inner world was allied to the rather Spanish handling of the paint. Such pictures, unpretentious, delightful, and able, allowed him to give the spontaneity he always sought after.

What continued to stir him was still life and landscape. Whereas his earlier ventures in the first genre had tended to be severe and formalistic, he now favoured a lighter, more decorative and 'painterly' treatment in which the plenitude and earthiness of the colours almost recalls the Neapolitans, a Ruoppolo, for instance. That he still retained some aspects of his earlier style may be seen in the *Still Life with Fruit and Flowers* (Fig. 80) in which he displayed his love for indicating the side of a table by means of a creamy line of paint or of using a delicate filigree of paint to indicate the wicker tracery of a basket. Yet he could also employ dashes of black and white paint to give merely the outline of a group of objects—the dynamic, dancing lines even suggest a note of hallucination. His final group of still life pictures, which are as yet insufficiently known, stress his status as one of the most varied masters of this genre in our time.

Nature, as ever, meant much to him and the series of landscapes painted at Chambourcy, at Donnemarie (1943) and on the Loire stress that he had lost none of his old touch. Yet his aims were different. Instead of attempting to render the scene naturalistically, he was anxious to suggest the drama that can be found in nature—as seen for instance, in *The Oppressive Landscape* (Fig. 86) or *The Little Cemetery*, 1946 (M. Pierre Lévy, Troyes); such pictures verge on the expressionistic in the sense that, even while suggesting the atmosphere, the mood given corresponds, one suspects, to his own outlook. What he was after was the evocation of a particular note and the depiction of the relationship between the elements and this he successfully caught in landscape sketches like the *Bacchantes* (Fig. 87), for instance, of 1945, where the dashes of white paint on black recall Magnasco.

All the same, he was still eager to give the feel of a precise place, and in a picture like the *Landscape on the banks of the Loire* (Fig. 82) his aim was not to translate the scene into terms depending for their relevance on the artist's imagination: rather he sought to give an exact image of it in identifiable terms. The keenness of his eye for tone came over in his disposition of the recessions: the trees are given their independence and the colours are successfully related to each other. In such works, anyone familiar with the parts of France he chose to paint must surely admit that he knew how to capture the essential character of his chosen district; and just as with Courbet's pictures of Ornans, we may find that the tones appearing in the canvas are discernible *in situ*—indeed to hold a piece of rock from Ornans close to a landscape by this artist is to be made aware of an exact correspondence—so the same is true when Derain's paintings of the Ile de France, Provence or Normandy are examined. He could also conjure up the magical element in his scene, as in the *Amiens* (Fig. 84) so that as the eye dwells on the soft, almost buttery paintings of the walls, the diffused light playing on the roof tops, and the small urgent figures, a note of mystery appears in the picture.

During the last part of his life, Derain was constantly engaged in theatrical design and with book illustration. In 1943, for instance, he completed his brilliant and colourful woodcuts for an edition of Rabelais's Pantagruel, published by Skira, in which his spontaneity and whimsicality were wonderfully well combined. He felt in close touch with the spirit of the book, and T. W. Earp once recalled an evening spent with the painter and Clive Bell in Paris, when he astonished them with his apt quotations. His liking for medieval themes—already shown in the early days—came across too in the charming illustrations for *Amis et Amille* which was posthumously published. His skill as a designer was equally well displayed in the sets for *Mam'zelle Angot*, a ballet with music by Charles Lecocq, orchestrated by Gordon Jacob, which was first performed by the Sadlers Wells Ballet Company at Covent Garden in 1947. Here he had the opportunity to bring together some of his favourite themes—figures of the Commedia dell'Arte and the popular types based on French revolutionary prints—and these were picked out with a bright colour that recalled the Fauve period. For the drop curtain he painted one of his typical landscapes—soft, undulating hills, touched in with blues, greys and greens. In these he managed to secure the spontaneity he always favoured—and nothing of this was lost when the small sketches were translated into the sets and costumes themselves. He was equally successful in the decors he undertook for Mozart's *Il Seraglio* (1951) and Rossini's *The Barber of Seville* (1952) which were performed at the musical festival at Aix-en-Provence.

Although he made various trips, notably to Noirmoutier in 1950 where he painted some vivid beach scenes like *Boats at Noirmoutier* (Fig. 85), Derain spent most of his time in Chambourcy, surrounded by his pictures by Corot, Cézanne and Renoir, and his collection of objects. He dwelt much on the conditions of the time and he was worried by the fact that too much education was harmful to those instinctive reactions so essential to artistic creation, a point he had made some years before in an interview with Herr Jedlicka. He felt too that his views on art, and his painting could not be properly understood unless his ideas on the problems of the twentieth century were taken into account. There was no denying, he maintained, that the world now derived an intense satisfaction from erecting a socialistic and communistic

47

structure in which the individual, with all his weakness and limitations, was dwarfed by the machinery of government; and this machinery in his opinion would become clogged by an excess of complications. 'Respect for the individual,' he declared, 'is all-important.' Above all, there must be room for those individuals who know how to enjoy. Indeed, enjoyment can only be retained as long as ideas or pursuits are followed with passion. His own aim in life had always been, and would continue to be, just this; and thus he strove, he said, to make his art expressive of his passion.

He felt certain that his art and his position were wrongly considered—just because he did not fit in. As he said:

'I am not attached to any principle—except that of liberty—but my idea of liberty is that it must be related to tradition. I do not wish to expound any theories as to what ought to be done in the arts. I simply paint as best I can. The point is that there are too many theories running around and not sufficient passion to make them work.'

And he made a similar point when, in his *L'Art de Peindre*, he declared that:

'Artists will never do anything with principles. Ideas are not enough: you need a miracle.'

Solitary, a trifle embittered, Derain's last years were not altogether happy and shortly after his final parting with Madame Derain, he was run over by a car at Chambourcy and died on the 8th September, 1954. Yet since his death, by one of these pleasing paradoxes that so delight the historian of taste, his contribution to contemporary art has taken on an added significance. It has begun to attract attention and discussion just because he understood certain of the problems now facing the younger generation. Already in the 1930's, men like Tal Coat, Humblot and Rohner, who formed the *Forces Nouvelles* group acknowledged his influence; that he stirred Balthus is apparent not only from his other work but from his revealing portrait of Derain, and both Gruber and Giacometti owed much to his example at specific moments in their careers. The latter in a remarkable tribute has confessed the extent to which his work intrigued and stimulated him, and to a greater degree than any of his contemporaries. He declared:

'All the routes, all the certitudes valid for, at least, the major bulk of the contemporary school, if not for them all, even including the abstract and tachiste painters, have no meaning for him. Where, therefore, can one find the means for expressing oneself? A red is not red, a line not a line, a volume not a volume; everything is contradictory, a bottomless pit in which one can founder. Yet, moreover, he only wanted to pin down some small part of the appearance of things, the wonderful, appealing and unknown appearance of what surrounds us.'

It was this aspect of his character that constantly compelled him to refer to the past when seeking an answer to the problems that were waiting to be solved; he felt, one may believe, as if he was after the philosopher's stone (and the occult always held a fascination for him) and that somewhere could be found the answer to his search. Allied to this trait was his aesthete's quest for artistic experience; African, Cypriot, and Roman art, early Italian painting, the French fifteenth-century school, Breughel, El Greco, Caravaggio, Rubens, and nearer to our own time, Corot, Renoir and Cézanne, were all examined and contributed something to his art. It was this side to his work, that has often embarrassed those who believe that art must strike out on a visibly new path.

Not even the warmest of his admirers, for instance, would choose to argue that he was an inventive artist in the sense that he was ever a discoverer of particularly new forms; he was not adventurous in this way—that after all was never his real aim. One must also acknowledge that the complexities of his mind and the diversity of his approach, his very prolixity, in fact, could lead him into temptations—certain of his fashionable portraits or female studies like *The Parisienne* (Private collection, Geneva) are apt to prove disconcerting. Moreover, in the 1920's, when he was so successful, he was sometimes prepared (usually out of kindness of heart) to release pictures which fall below his best standard, and he was inclined to dash off casual studies, usually of female models, which, for all their craftsmanship, lack bite. His failures must indeed be admitted.

Nor is it always possible to see how his own work expressed the principles set forth in his statements. He insisted so strongly on instinctive painting and on the need for spontaneity; however, many of his pictures, and by no means the worst, seem to embody quite different characteristics. His ambition did not always survive in his art. It could be that he dispersed himself in too many directions and peripheral projects—book illustrations, ballet designs, minor canvases. But yet, especially in his ballet designs, he revealed his breadth of vision and his dexterity. Such activities may have been the consequence of his own sense of failure. It is hard not to feel that besides being commissioned to design for the ballet and illustrate books, he should have been asked to paint, for instance, a fresco for a chapel or a public building. This would have compelled him to coordinate all his forces into one major effort. In this respect, the modern painter is often at a disadvantage in comparison with his predecessors; he is allowed to paint what he wishes, as he wishes, whereas in the past he was often requested to adhere to a libretto, and if Derain had been placed in this position, his gifts for organisation, for solid draughtsmanship and for compositional firmness might have flowered more than was the case.

One wonders if Derain ought to be considered not only as a painter in his own right but as a symbolic figure. Is he not one of those men (they exist at all generations) who believe in the conservative principle, and that an artist ought to base his work on a continuation of earlier styles? T. S. Eliot has observed that:

'Tradition cannot be inherited, and if you want it you must obtain it by great labour. It involves, in the first place, the historical sense, which we may call nearly indispensable to anyone who would continue to be a poet beyond his twenty-fifth year; and the historical sense involves a perception, not only of the pastness of the past, but of its presence; the historical sense compels a man to write not merely with his own generation in his bones, but with a feeling that the whole of the literature of Europe from Homer and within it the whole of the literature of his own country has a simultaneous order. This historical sense which is a sense of the timeless as well as of the temporal and of the timeless and of the temporal together, is what makes a writer traditional. And it is at the same time what makes a writer most acutely conscious of his place in time, of his own contemporaneity.'

Derain's recognition of the relevance of tradition was one of his main assets. He realised that no one particular approach to painting, no single solution, however valuable and brilliant, persists for ever and enjoys a permanent priority: and that in our era, as in the past, there is room, ample room even, for different and contradictory conventions. He understood that each specific subject called for a different approach. The question which has to be asked, and which it may still be too early to answer, is whether or not Derain succeeded in incorporating in his work the historical sense, as understood by Mr. Eliot; was he able, in fact, to make tradition, his conception of tradition, significant for his own generation?

It is the challenge implicit in his position that makes any precise estimate of Derain's position in contemporary art so extremely difficult. Naturally enough, his prowess as a Fauve, and as one of the most delicious colourists of the 1900's, is not in dispute. Yet opinions are sharply divided as to the value of his work after the 1920's, and in particular in respect of those paintings produced at the end of his life. Was his adherence to tradition feasible at a time when the whole nature of art had been revolutionised? Can any pleasure be derived from his art, as a consequence of this apparent limitation? But it is just because there is no very evident or valid idea of academic excellence, no criterion that is universally acceptable or accepted, that Derain's decision to go his own way—even if that way was opposed to many of his colleagues—is *valid*. It seems to me, as I pointed out at the start of this study, that one can only go by one's own reactions in front of specific canvases. If they provide one with an aesthetic experience, the works themselves must be considered (within the boundaries imposed by an individual's sensibility) as of merit.

While it would be wrong-headed to argue that all the works produced by Derain in his latter years were of equal quality, the dismissal of his final period as being insignificant is not acceptable: virtue may be found in his still life and landscape, where he could indulge his love of instinctive painting. In any valuation of his art at this period—as of his work as a whole—one must reckon with the difficulty, if not impossibility, of accurately determining the status of an artist who is still close to us. As with any contemporary artist, one's evaluation of his status, in fact, is no more than approximative—and posterity will accept or reject, and doubtless modify, the views reached in our own era. Perhaps, at this stage, one can do no more than present the problems presented by his painting, and suspend judgement.

In any event, Derain's appeal at the present time may be accounted for by another reason; that is his awareness, acute and consistent, of the tragic sense of life. He was, as Ozenfant once termed him, 'a disenchanted optimist'. This note was frequently sounded in his paintings—the gaunt *Two Sisters* (Fig. 39), the sparse still life pictures, the silent austere landscapes of his later years—all expressed his point of view. He had perhaps his share of the belief in *l'absurde*, which Camus analysed so well and sharply, and as M. Alain Robbe-Grillet has pointed out, this absurdity 'turns out to be a form of tragic humanism'. It may even be that his passion for objects, for the past, for stability, was all the stronger just because he believed in Pascal's definition of the 'natural misery of our condition'. His quest for permanence was all the more obsessive just because he realised that he could not reach the goal he sought.

This disenchantment, this awareness of the limitations, perpetual and gnaw-ing, of our efforts, this desire for faith and fundamental absence of it (except perhaps in respect to his own work, and then only on occasion), this dislike and suspicion of the contemporary world, at times exaggerated and even irritating, this introspective and complex mentality, seemed to be at variance with the man as he appeared to the outside world. He might look so easy to read, deceptively easy, one ought to add; but the large, imposing, robust if slightly run-down figure (as he appeared in the last years) reminded one of a warm and comfortable country house, which had known better days.

He was ill adjusted to the modern world. Of this there can be little doubt and that this was so, may be attributed to his particular and fundamentally dangerous attitude to life. He believed that no sensation ought to be refused, no experience rejected if it appealed to him—just because by refusing such challenges one risked losing the chance of really understanding what life and art were about; he was eager to pierce to the essentials at all costs. The consequence of this approach, essentially that of an aesthete and a sensualist, was his availability to all that went on. It was this willingness or rather eagerness to embrace both the aesthetic and the physical and to go the whole length, that made him so susceptible to outside influences. He had the roving eye. But he embarked on such adventures, with a conscious deliberation, in order to find out all he could; but the deceptions occasioned by his restlessness must have been compensated for by the variety of his experiences.

A brilliant talker, a realist with curious naiveté, a *frondeur*, Derain was ever paradoxical. He was a man of the Renaissance endowed with splendid appetites. Yet his very sensitivity to mood, his rejection of superficial hedonism, though his love for it was not to be denied, his incompatibility, and his dislike for conformism give him the fascination of a man who had his failures as well as his successes. He knew well that, compared to the past, the difficulties of capturing the initial shock of recognition were considerable. He once said that everyone ought to find the wine that suits him: that a wine exists for every palette. 'Have you found yours?' he was asked. '*Non,*' was the reply. This decisive comment gave the man; it was a comment on human imperfectibility and the transience of systems; and this very dissatisfaction, this search for the unaffected, permitted him to produce, on occasion, a picture or a drawing which stays in the memory.

NOTES TO THE INTRODUCTION

page 6, line 24. See brochure, *Chatou*, issued at the time of the exhibition with this title at the Galerie Bing, Paris, 1947. p. 2.

p. 6, l. 37. op. cit. p. 2.

p. 7, l. 3. *Lettres à Vlaminck*, ed. M. Vlaminck, 1955, . 112.

p. 7, l. 8. 'Propos de Derain' collected by Madame Pierre Lévy in *Prisme des Arts*, November, 1956, pp. 2–6.

p. 7, l. 12. Cited by Alfred Barr, *Matisse and His Public*, 1951, p. 42.

p. 7, l. 12. See Georges Duthuit, 'Le Fauvisme', in *Cahiers d'Art*, IV. 1929. p. 268.

p. 7, l. 16. Daniel Henry, *Derain*, 1920. p. 3.

p. 7, l. 34. For an account of Derain's days with Vlaminck at Chatou, see M. Vlaminck, *Tournant Dangereux*, 1929, passim.

p. 8, l. 2. See J. Leymarie, *Fauvism*, 1959, repr. p. 40.

p. 8, l. 16. *Chatou*, p. 4.

p. 8, l. 25. Vlaminck, op. cit. p. 21.

p. 8, l. 27. *Chatou*, p. 4.

p. 8, l. 32. John Rewald, *Les Fauves*, 1952, repr. p. 22.

p. 8, l. 34. *Chatou*, repr. p. 5.

p. 8, l. 37. See Georges Duthuit, 'Le Fauvisme', in *Cahiers d'Art*, IV 1929. repr. pp. 265 and 267.

p. 8, l. 39. *Cahiers d'Art*, v., 1930 repr. p. 129. It was for long attributed to Benedetto Ghirlandajo (see Louis Hautecoeur in his catalogue of the Louvre (no. 1323.)) Van Marle and Berenson have given to to G. B. Utili while Wart Arslan ascribed it to Biagio d'Antonio. Derain asked for authorisation to copy the picture on the 24th January, 1901, and finished it by the 28th April. (Information from Madame Jean Adhémar.)

p. 8, l. 42. *Cahiers d'Art*, op. cit. p. 268.

p. 9, l. 11. Cited by Alfred Barr, op. cit. p. 42.

p. 9, l. 21. Alfred Barr, op. cit. repr. p. 66.

p. 9, l. 22. Alfred Barr, op. cit. repr. p. 304.

p. 9, l. 35. *The Portrait of a Soldier* (? Self-Portrait) in the Dikran Khan Kelekian sale, American Art Association, New York, 30–31 January, 1923 (42, repr.), was presumably painted at this date.

p. 10, l. 21. *Lettres*, p. 26.

p. 10, l. 39. *Lettres*, Introduction, p. 9.

p. 11, l. 8. *Lettres*, p. 95.

p. 11, l. 10. *Lettres*, p. 98.

p. 11, l. 24. *Lettres*, p. 43.

p. 11, l. 32. *Lettres*, p. 108.

p. 12, l. 10. 'Picasso et la Poésie', in *Commentari*, IV, 1953, pp. 187–188; for an interesting essay on the intellectual cross-currents at this time, see Phoebe Pool 'Sources and Background of Picasso's Art 1900–1906' in *The Burlington Magazine*, CI, May, 1959, pp. 176–182.

p. 12, l. 19. *Lettres*, p. 27.

p. 12, l. 21. *Lettres*, p. 57.

p. 12, l. 26. *Lettres*, p. 60.

p. 12, l. 33. *Lettres*, p. 62.

p. 13, l. 2. *Lettres*, p. 40.

p. 13, l. 4. *Lettres*, p. 63.

p. 13, l. 9. *Lettres*, p. 107.

p. 13, l. 18. *Lettres*, p. 116.

p. 13, l. 29. See 'XX Century French Painters', Lefevre Gallery, London, March, 1958 (5, repr.).

p. 13, l. 35. See Denys Sutton, 'André Derain: Art as Fate', in *Encounter*, October, 1955, p. 74.

p. 14, l. 33. See Gertrud Stein, *The Autobiography of Alice B. Toklas*, 1933, p. 46.

p. 14, l. 37. 'Propos de Derain'. op. cit.

p. 14, l. 39. See Ronald Alley, *Tate Gallery, Foreign Paintings, Drawings and Sculptures*, 1959, pp. 66 and 149–150.

p. 15, l. 2. Alfred Barr, op. cit. p. 70.

p. 15, l. 3. Alfred Barr, op. cit. p. 73.

p. 15, l. 8. John Rewald, op. cit. repr. p. 21.

p. 15, l. 9. John Rewald, op. cit. repr. p. 23.

p. 15, l. 19. *Fauvism*, 1959, p. 81.

p. 15, l. 21. Alfred Barr, op. cit. p. 317.

p. 15, l. 29. See Michel Puy, *Jean Puy*, 1920, repr. p. 27.

p. 15, l. 30. Alfred Barr, op cit. p. 320.

p. 15, l. 32. See 'Maîtres de l'Art Indépendant', Petit Palais Paris, 1937 (16, repr.).

p. 16, l. 2. Review of Alfred Barr, *Matisse, his Art and his Public*, in *The Art Bulletin*, xxxiv, September, 1952 (3), p. 248.

p. 16, l. 10. Alfred Barr, op. cit. p. 123.

p. 16, l. 15. Alfred Barr, op. cit. pp. 119–123.

p. 16, l. 36. *Lettres*, pp. 154–155.

p. 17, l. 2. See Charles Sterling, *Great French Paintings in the Hermitage*, 1958, repr. p. 109 in colour.

p. 17, l. 9. Cited in *L'Illustration*, November, 1905. For a convenient reproduction of this page, see Alfred Barr, op. cit. p. 19.

p. 17, l. 20. Jean Leymarie, *Fauvism*, 1959, p. 68.

p. 17, l. 23. Leymarie, op. cit. repr. p. 68.

p. 17, l. 25. *Recollections of a Picture Dealer*, 1936, p. 201.

p. 17, l. 27. Ronald Alley, op. cit. pp. 64–65.

p. 17, l. 29. Alley, op. cit.

p. 17, l. 38. See 'Derain', London, 1957 (11).

p. 17, l. 39. See 'Derain', London, 1957 (12).

p. 17, l. 40. See 'La Collection Lehman de New York', L'Orangerie, Paris, 1957 (66).

p. 18, l. 6. *Lettres*, p. 155.

p. 18, l. 10. *Lettres*, p. 196.

p. 18, l. 11. See Denys Sutton, 'André Derain: Art as Fate', in *Encounter*, October, 1955, p. 69.

p. 18, l. 18. *Lettres*, p. 196.

p. 18, l. 20. M. Raynal, A. Rudlinger, H. Bolliger, J. Lassaigne, *Histoire de la Peinture Moderne*, 1950, repr. p. 39 (in colour).

p. 18, l. 23. *The Fauvist Painters*, 1950, p. 48.

p. 18, l. 37. For a list of the pictures he sent to the Salon des Indépendants and to the Salon d'Automne between 1905 and 1910, see 'Derain', London, 1957, pp. xxviii–xxix.

p. 19, l. 6. *Lettres*, p. 146.

p. 19, l. 13. Jean Leymarie, *Fauvism*, 1959, p. 81.

p. 19, l. 31. *Lettres*, p. 188.

p. 19, l. 34. Repr. Duthuit, op. cit. plate 27.

p. 20, l. 3. Jean Leymarie, *Fauvism*, 1959, p. 125.

p. 20, l. 32. Cited by Georges Duthuit, op. cit. p. 29.

p. 20, l. 33. Duthuit, op. cit., p. 29.

p. 21, l. 11. Duthuit, op. cit., p. 29.

p. 21, l. 15. John Rewald, *Les Fauves*, 1950, p. 24.

p. 21, l. 28. *The Autobiography of Alice B. Toklas*, 1933, p. 46.

p. 21, l. 33. *Picasso et Ses Amis*, 1933, p. 72.

p. 21, l. 38. See Guy Habasque for an informative note on this mask in *Les Soirées de Paris*, Galerie Knoedler, Paris, 1958. no. 36.

p. 22, l. 11. For a valuable account of *Les Demoiselles d'Avignon* (Museum of Modern Art, New York), see Roland Penrose, *Picasso*, 1958. pp. 121-148.

p. 22, l. 22. Daniel Henry, *Derain*, 1920. Plate 3.

p. 22, l. 25. Daniel Henry, op cit., Plate 9.

p. 22, l. 27. Ibid. pp. 4-5.

p. 22, l. 35. 'Memorial', Paris, 1954-1955 (142, Plate XIX).

p. 22, l. 35. See Carl Einstein, *Die Kunst des 20 Jahrhunderts*, 1926, repr. p. 217.

p. 23, l. 15. Galerie Kahnweiler, No. 2122.

p. 23, l. 33. 'Sammlung Rupf', Kunstmuseum, Berne, 1956 (20, repr.).

p. 23, l. 36. Exh: 'Derain', Charpentier, Paris, 1955 (ii, repr.).

p. 23, l. 37. Henry R. Hope, *Georges Braque*, 1949, p. 30.

p. 23, l. 40. Daniel Henry, op. cit. plate 8.

p. 24, l. 2. *Lettres*, p. 206.

p. 24, l. 9. *Lettres*, p. 176.

p. 24, l. 20. *Lettres*, p. 178.

p. 24, l. 30. *Le Temps*, 14 October, 1912, p. 5, cited by Guy Habasque in *Les Soirées de Paris*, Galerie Knoedler, Paris. 1958 No. 10, bis. See 'Derain', Charpentier, 1955 (12, repr.).

p. 24, l. 40. *Les Etapes de La Peinture Française Contemporaine*, 1944, vol. II, p. 168.

p. 26, l. 6. See 'Sammlung Rupf', Kunstmuseum, Berne, 1956, (23, Plate VIII).

p. 26, l. 10. Malcolm Vaughan, *Derain*, 1941. pp. 55-56.

p. 26, l. 32. *Lettres*, p. 204.

p. 27, l. 17. J. P. Crespelle, *Vlaminck fauve de la peinture*, 1958, pp. 177-178.

p. 27, l. 22. Daniel Henry, op. cit. Plate 94a.

p. 28, l. 13. *Lettres*, p. 172.

p. 28, l. 14. See *Pour ou Contre André Derain*, 1931 repr. Plate iv.

p. 28, l. 15. Galerie Kahnweiler, Nos. 2043, 2048, 2051.

p. 28, l. 16. Henry R. Hope, op. cit. repr. p. 48.

p. 28, l. 18. *Twentieth Century French Paintings from the Chester Dale Collection*, 1952, repr. p. 19.

p. 28, l. 38. See 'Sammlung Rupf', op. cit. (26, repr. p. 15).

p. 29, l. 4. C. Zervos, *Histoire de l'Art Contemporain*, 1938, repr. p. 181.

p. 29, l. 12. *La petite fille* (Galerie Kahnweiler, no. 2191) and *Femme assise dans un fanteuil* (Galerie Kahnweiler, no. 2190): the latter, which is in the Soviet State Collection, is repr. C. Zervos, op. cit. p. 181.

p. 29, l. 23. A. Basler, *Derain* (Druet), 1929, Plate II.

p. 29, l. 36. Daniel Henry, op. cit. Plate 28.

p. 29, l. 38. 'Maîtres de l'Art Indépendant, Petit Palais, Paris, 1936 (16, repr.).

p. 31, l. 24. *Speculations*, 1924, p. 93.

p. 31, l. 27. Daniel Henry, op. cit. Plate 25.

p. 31, l. 37. *L'Art Vivant*, 1920, pp. 75-82.

p. 32, l. 14. For a reprint of the French text, see 'Derain' London, 1957, pp xxvii-xxviii.

p. 32, l. 21. *Lettres*, p. 218.

p. 32, l. 26. *Lettres*, p. 221.

p. 32, l. 30. Carl Einstein, op. cit. repr, p. 218.

p. 32, l. 36. *Lettres*, p. 221.

p. 32, l. 40. In the collection of Monsieur Renou, Paris; see 'Memorial', Paris, 1954-1955, (37). A flower piece, given to 1918, was exhibited Derain, Galerie Maeght, Paris, 1958 (26).

p. 32, l. 41. A fragment, entitled *L'Annonce faite à Marie*, is in the collection of Madame Derain: see 'Memorial', (No. 38).

p. 33, l. 22. *Complete Book of Ballets*, 1949, pp. 880-882. See also Clive Bell, *Old Friends*, 1956, pp. 171-172.

p. 34, l. 5. See 'Derain' London, 1957 (18); for Derain's pictures in the Post Impressionist exhibitions, see also Benedict Nicolson 'Post Impressionism and Roger Fry' in *The Burlington Magazine*, XLIII, 1957, pp. 11-15.

p. 34, l. 32. Published in 1920. An English edition was published in New York, 1951, London, 1956, New York edition, p. 4.

p. 36, l. 15. 'The Authority of M. Derain' in *Since Cézanne*, 1922, p. 211.

p. 36, l. 29. *Lettres*, p. 223.

p. 36, l. 32. Daniel Henry, op. cit. Plate 30.

p. 36, l. 33. Daniel Henry, op. cit. Plate 31.

p. 36, l. 40. Adolphe Basler, *Derain*, 1931, Plate 5.

p. 36, l. 41. Carl Einstein, op. cit. repr. p. 209.

p. 38. l. 1. cf. *Formes*, XXI, 1933, repr. opp. p. 378.

p. 38, l. 8. 'Propos de Derain', op. cit. p. 3.

p. 38, l. 14. *Les Pas Perdus*, 1924, pp. 105-112.

p. 38, l. 31. In *Commune*, no. 21, reprinted in *De la Palette à L'Ecritoire*, ed. André Lhote, 1946, pp. 393-595.

p. 39, l. 11. *Propos d'Artistes*, 1925, p. 42.

p. 40, l. 1. 'Derain', London, 1957 (47).

p. 41, l. 21. *Derain*, 1948, p. 6.

p. 42, l. 6. See Duncan Phillips, 'A modern masterpiece by Derain', in *Phillips Memorial Gallery*, 1929, pp. 30-33 (repr.).

p. 42, l. 19. For Derain's palette, see *Pour ou Contre*, op. cit. p. 15.

p. 43, l. 27. Clive Bell, *Old Friends*, 1956, pp. 166-190.

p. 43, l. 27. *L'Ami des Peintres*, 1944, passim.

p. 43, l. 29. See Catalogue of the Salon d'Automne, Paris, 1955, pp. 24-25.

p. 44, l. 4. *Pour ou Contre*, op. cit. p. 4.

p. 44, l. 7. Ibid, p.8.

p. 44, l. 27. 'Memorial', Paris, 1954-1955 (83)

p. 44, l. 39. Derain, London, 1957 (65, repr.).

p. 46, l. 2. 'Memorial', Paris, 1954-1955.

p. 47, l. 38. 'Begegnung mit André Derain' in *Begegnungen mit Künstlern der Gegenwart*, 1945, pp. 112-132.

p. 47, l. 41. Denys Sutton, 'André Derain: Art as Fate' in *Encounter*, October, 1955, pp. 68-72.

p. 48, l. 16. Cited in 'Memorial', Paris, 1954-1955, p. 14.

p. 48, l. 39. In *Derrière le Miroir* (Galerie Maeght), February-March, 1957.

p. 49, l. 16. See 'Derain', Galerie Motte, Geneva, 1955 (10, repr. pl 13).

p. 50, l. 2. 'Tradition and the Individual Talent' written in 1917; in *Points of View*, edited John Hayward, 1941. p. 25.

p. 51, l. 12. *Pour ou Contre*, op. cit. p. 7.

p. 51, l. 17. See Alain Robbe-Grillet, 'Old Values and the New Novel' in *The London Magazine*, February, 1959. p. 42.

PLATES

PLATES.

I SELF-PORTRAIT. About 1895-1899

2 THE ROAD TO CARRIÈRES. 1899

3 THE FUNERAL. About 1899

4 THE BALL AT SURESNES. 1903

5 THE DANCER. 1906

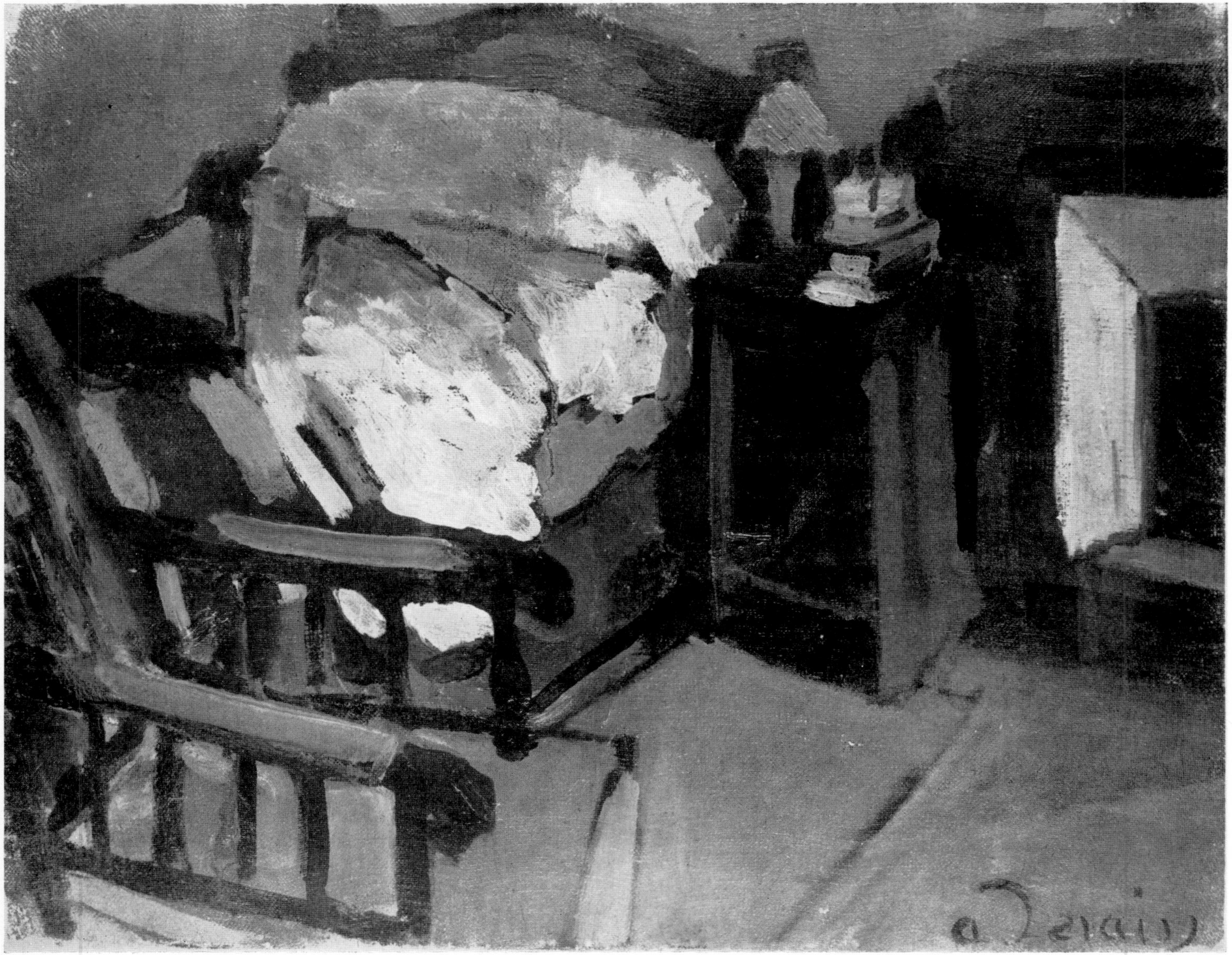

6 THE BEDROOM. About 1900–01

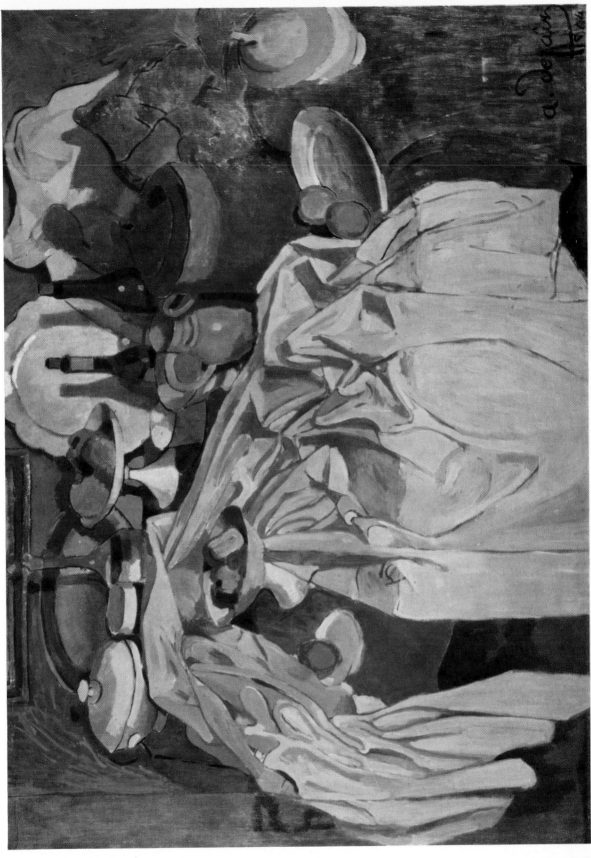

7 STILL LIFE.
1904

8 SNOWSCAPE AT CHATOU. About 1904

9 THE BRIDGE AT LE PECQ. 1904

10 VINEYARDS IN SPRING. About 1906

11 COLLIOURE. 1905

12 THE HOUSES OF PARLIAMENT.
1905-1906

13 HYDE PARK. About 1906

14 THE GOLDEN AGE. About 1905

15 THE DANCE. About 1905-6

6 TURNING ROAD, L'ESTAQUE. 1905

17 LANDSCAPE AT CASSIS.
1906

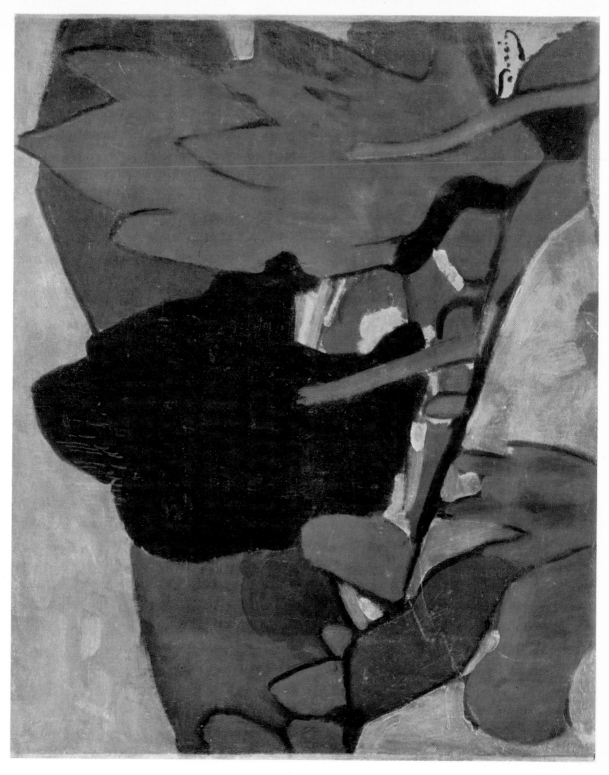

18 LANDSCAPE AT CASSIS.
About 1907

19 NUDE FIGURES. 1907

20 THE BATHERS. 1908

21 THE RED HOUSE. 1909

22

23

26 STILL LIFE. 1910

27 STILL LIFE. 1912

28 THE ROAD AT CAMIERS. 1911

29 THE CHURCH AT VERS 1912

INSIDE THE FOREST. About 1912

31 THE FOREST. 1912

32 THE BAGPIPER. 1911

33 CALVARY. 1912

34 YOUNG GIRL. 1914

35 PORTRAIT OF ITURRINO. 1914

36 THE OFFERING. 1913

37 THE GAME-BAG. 1913

38 VIEW OF MARTIGUES. 1913

39 THE TWO SISTERS. 1914

40 THE LAST SUPPER. 1913

41 THE DRINKERS. 1913-14

42 SATURDAY. 1911-14

43 'CHEVALIER X'. 1914

44 STILL LIFE IN FRONT OF A WINDOW. 1912

45 HEAD OF A GIRL. 1920

46 THE ARTIST IN HIS STUDIO. 1920-21

47 THE ITALIAN MODEL. 1921-22

48 THE ROAD AT ALBANO. 1921

49 A VILLAGE IN PROVENCE. About 1921-22

50 NEAR CASTEL GANDOLFO. 1921

51 WOODLAND SCENE AT OLLIOULES.
1921-22

52 FLOWERPIECE. About 1924

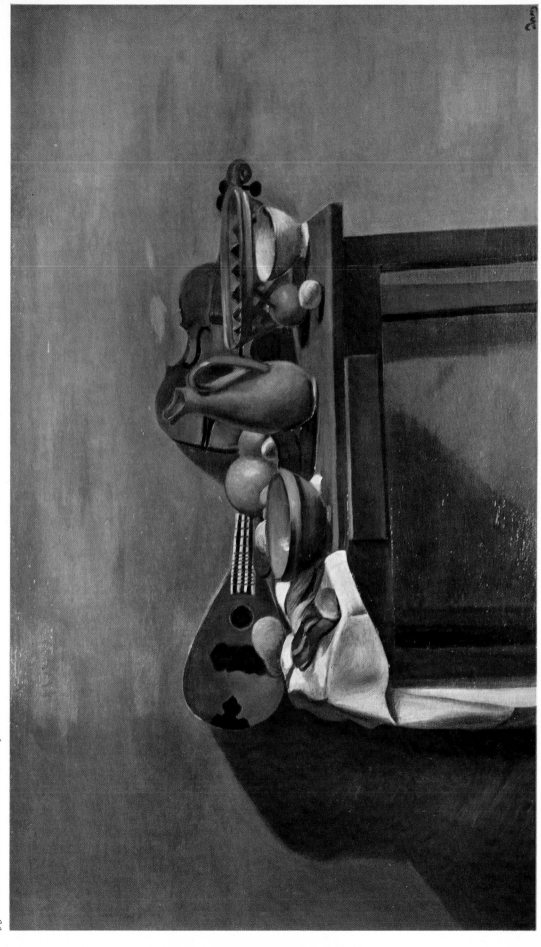

53 THE LADEN TABLE. About 1921-22

54 VASE OF ROSES WITH PLATE AND PIPE. About 1923-25

55 THE BEAUTIFUL MODEL. 1923

56 HARLEQUIN. About 1924

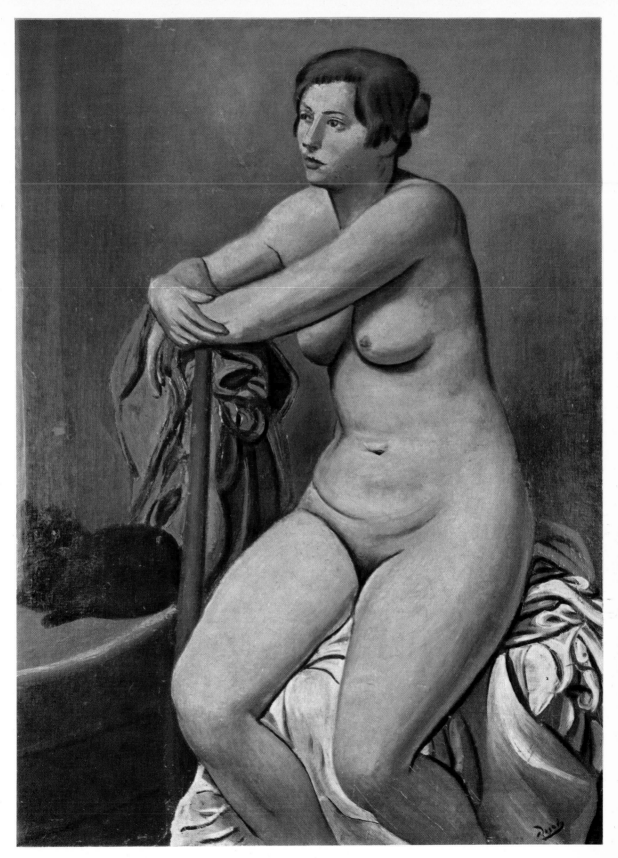

57 NUDE WITH A CAT. 1921-23

58 WOMAN IN A CHEMISE. About 1928

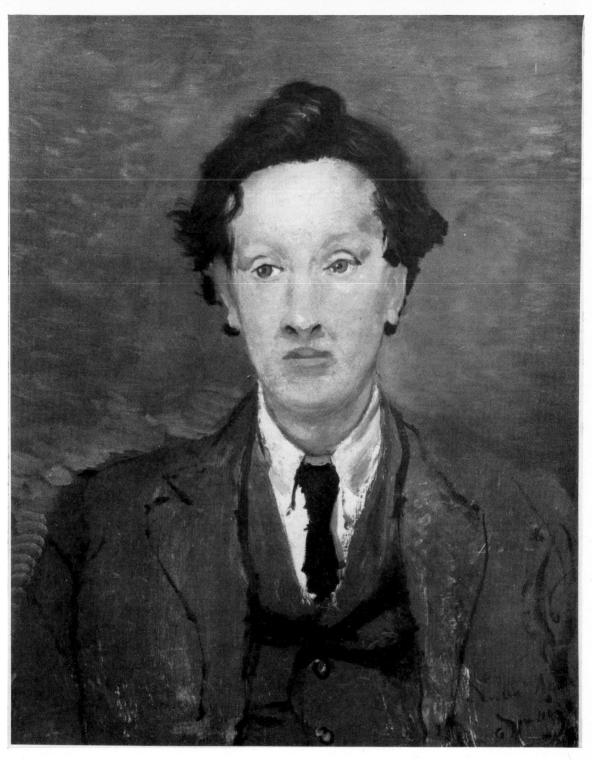

59 PORTRAIT OF VINCENT MUSELLI. 1925

60 HARLEQUIN. Pencil Drawing, 1924

61 PIERROT AND HARLEQUIN. 1924

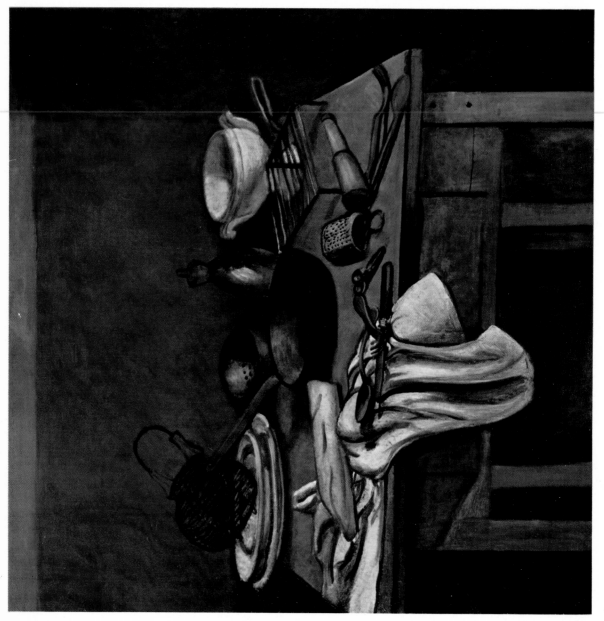

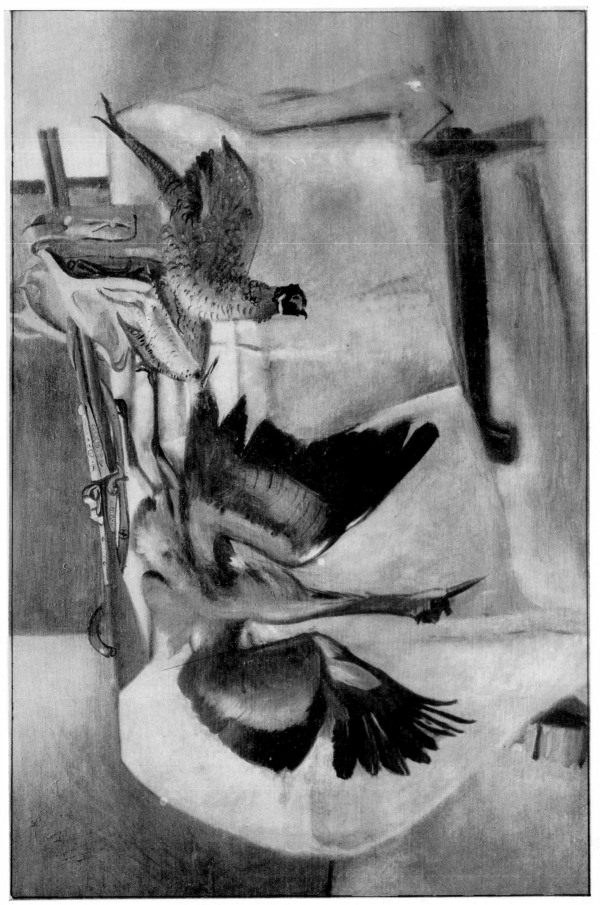

63 STILL LIFE: DEAD GAME. About 1928

64 HARLEQUIN WITH GUITAR. 1924

65 THE LARGE NUDE. 1928-29

66 GENEVIÈVE. 1931

67 THE BLONDE ITALIAN. About 1930

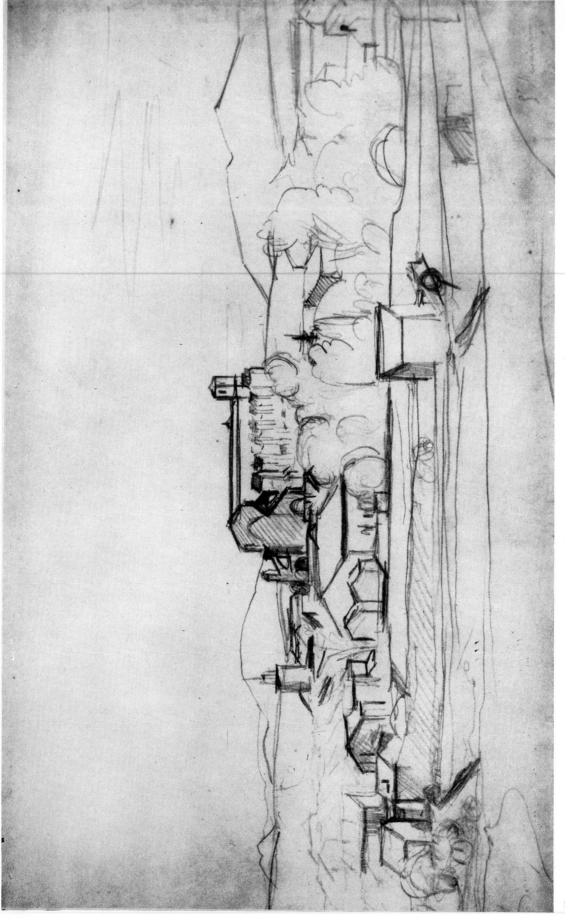

69 THE BASILICA OF ST. MAXIMIN.
1930

70 THE FOUNTAIN AT OLIÈRES. 1930

71 THE GLADE. 1931

72 TWO NUDES WITH FRUIT. About 1935

73 THE SURPRISE. 1938

74 STAG HUNT. About 1938

75 THE PAINTER WITH HIS FAMILY. About 1939

76 THE DRUMMER BOY. 1945

77 THE DEPORTEE. About 1941

78 FLOWERS IN A VASE. 1932

79 STILL LIFE. 1938-39

80 STILL LIFE WITH FRUIT AND FLOWERS. About 1945

81 STILL LIFE ON BLACK GROUND. About 1945

82 LANDSCAPE ON THE BANKS OF THE LOIRE. About 1942

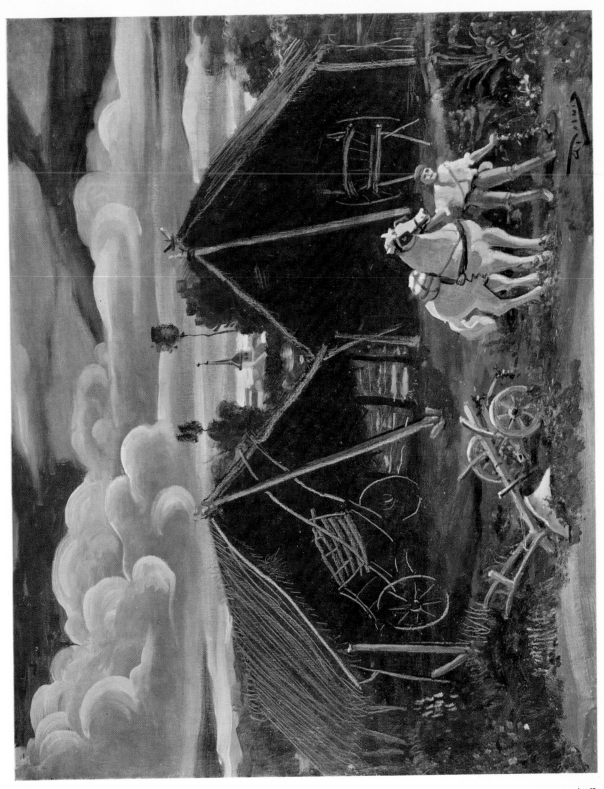

83 THE TWO SHEDS.
About 1943

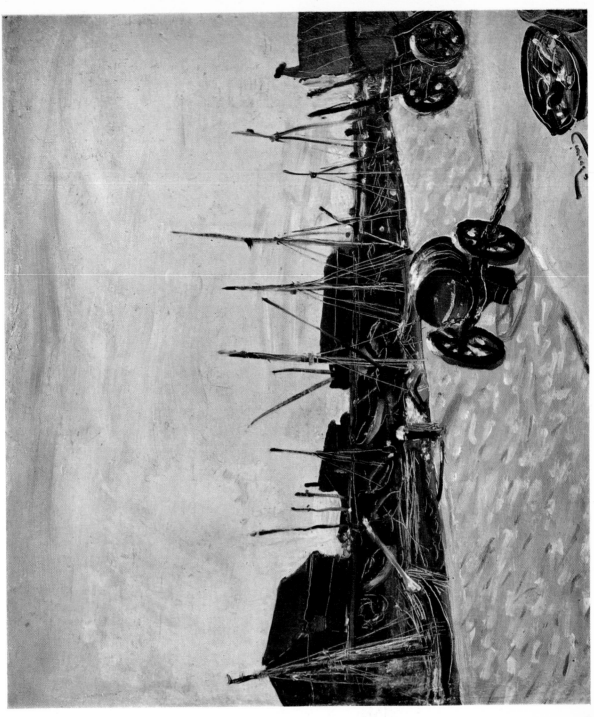

85 BOATS AT NOIRMOUTIER. 1950

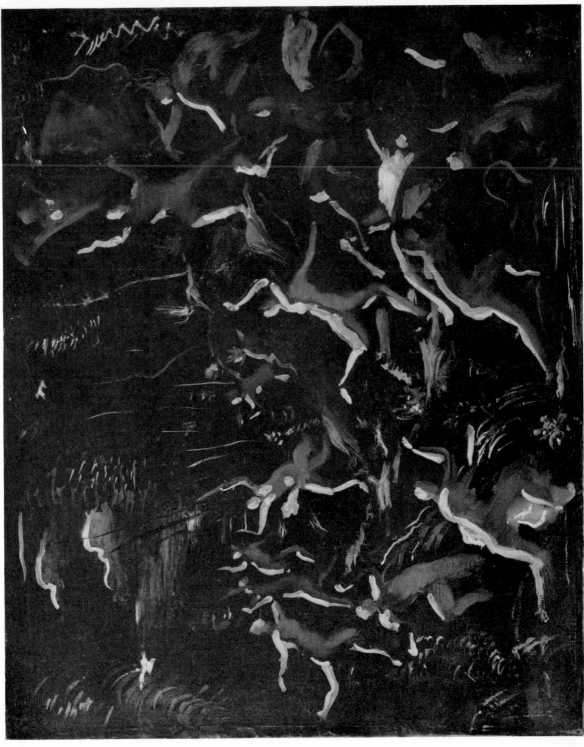

88 DESIGN FOR THE BALLET MAM'ZELLE ANGOT   1945

BIOGRAPHICAL CHRONOLOGY

BIBLIOGRAPHY

NOTES ON THE ILLUSTRATIONS

ACKNOWLEDGEMENTS

BIOGRAPHICAL CHRONOLOGY

1880   10 June. André Derain born at Chatou, the son of a well to do pastry cook. Attends the school of Sainte Croix, Le Vésinet, and later the Lycée Chaptal, Paris.

c.1895   Begins to paint. At some date around this period received lessons from Jacomin, a friend of Cézanne's.

1896   Attends the Ecole des Mines at Paris.

1898-9   Studies at the Académie Carrière, Paris. Visits Brittany.

1899   Again visits Brittany.

1900   July. Meets Vlaminck. At this date shared a studio with Vlaminck in an old disused restaurant on the Seine. Paints at Chatou, Le Pecq, St Germain-en-laye, and Carrières-Saint-Denis. Copies Old Masters in the Louvre with Linaret and Puy. In autumn and new year paints copy after 'Ghirlandajo's' *Christ Carrying the Cross*. Meets Henri Matisse. According to Vlaminck was already contributing illustrations to the Paris press.

1901   Visits the Van Gogh exhibition at Bernheim-Jeune, Paris, where introduces Vlaminck to Matisse. Spends summer at Belle-Ile in Brittany. In autumn begins military service at Commercy.

1902   In 1902 or 1903 paints a series of decorations for the barracks at Commercy which were subsequently white-washed. Undertakes illustrations for *Le Rire* and *Le Sourire* under the pseudonym of 'Bouzi'. Illustrates Vlaminck's and F. Sernanda's *D'un Lit à l'autre*. Begins a long correspondence with Vlaminck.

1903   Illustrates Vlaminck's *Tout pour ça*. Paints *Le Bal à Suresnes* (Fig. 4) signed and dated 1903, now in the St Louis Museum. In this year or 1904 takes an interest in Negro art, probably through Vlaminck.

1904   Finishes his period of military service. Matisse persuades his parents to allow Derain to become a full-time painter. Studies at the Académie Julian against the advice of Vlaminck. Paints *Still Life* (Fig. 7) signed and dated 1904, in the collection of Madame Baron. Paints *Les Péniches* at Le Pecq; also works at Montesson and Marly. Probably meets Guillaume Apollinaire this year.

1905   In February Ambroise Vollard, who was introduced to Derain by Matisse, buys his studio and places him under contract. Exhibits at the Salon des Indépendants, on the suggestion of Matisse. Sells four pictures there for 50 francs each; sent by his father to Collioure, where in July and August works with Matisse. Matisse painted Derain's portrait now in Tate Gallery. Vlaminck paints his portrait. Also visits L'Estaque and Marseilles. Returns to Paris in September. Exhibits at the Salon d'Automne in the famous 'Fauve' exhibition. Visits London for the first time and presumably paints some of his Thames series. Lives at 7 Place de l'Hôtel de Ville at Chatou. Probably begins to execute ceramic designs for Vollard and Metthey.

1906   Visits London in the spring and paints several of his Thames series. Paints at Le Havre. Probably visits L'Estaque. Becomes a friend of Picasso. Exhibits at the Salon des Indépendants, the Salon d'Automne, and at the Galerie Berthe Weill.

1907   Called up for military service again; spends twenty-eight days in the army. Visits Cassis. With Picasso at Avignon. Kahnweiler places him under contract. Executes stone sculpture. Marries in October and moves from Chatou to 'Les Fusains', 22 rue Tourlaque, Montmartre. Exhibits at the Salon des Indépendants, Salon d'Automne, and at Galerie Berthe Weill. Destroys part of his production in the autumn of 1907 or early in 1908.

1908   Makes a new circle of friends in Montmartre; in constant touch with Picasso, Braque, Van Dongen, and Vlaminck. Spends from May to end of November at Martigues. Braque at L'Estaque. Paints *The Bathers* (Fig. 20) and *The Toilet*. Exhibits at Salon des Indépendants, Salon d'Automne, Galeries Weill and Druet.

1909   Paints landscapes at Montreuil and at Neuville on the Somme. Spends summer at Carrières-Saint-Denis (with Braque). Death of his father in autumn. Exhibits at the Salon des Indépendants. Executes woodcuts for Apollinaire's *L'Enchanteur Pourrissant*, published by D. H. Kahnweiler.

1910   Paints at Villeneuve Loubat and Cagnes: *The Old Bridge at Cagnes* (Fig. 22). Visits Cadaquès in Spain with Picasso. Visits London with his mother. Spends winter at Boulogne and Etaples. Leaves Montmartre for 13 rue Bonaparte on the

Left Bank. Exhibits at the Salon des Indépendants. In October-January 1911, represented by three pictures in the 'Manet and the Post-Impressionists' Exhibition at the Grafton Galleries.

1911   Visits Beauvais, Serbonne-sur-le-Grand Morin and Camiers in the Pas de Calais, where he paints *The Bagpiper* (Fig. 32). Also paints still life.

1912   Visits Le Vers in the Lot. Paints *Calvary* (Fig. 33), *The Church at Vers* (Fig. 29), *The Offering* (Fig. 36). Illustrates Max Jacob's *Les Œuvres burlesques et mystiques de Frère Matorel, mort au couvent*, published by D. H. Kahnweiler. Spends autumn in Paris.

Dec. 1912 to Jan. 1913   Represented by six pictures in the 'Second Post-Impressionist' Exhibition at the Grafton Galleries, London.

1913   Paints series of still life pictures. Spends summer at Martigues (la Villa Paradis), where Vlaminck visits him with his family for a week. Begins to paint forest scenes, not after nature but in the studio in Paris.

1914   Paints *The Last Supper* (Fig. 40), *Saturday* (Fig. 42), *Portrait of Chevalier X* (Fig. 43), *The Two Sisters* (Fig. 37). Exhibits: January-February, Neue Galerie, Berlin; Spring, exhibits Alfred Flechtheim, Dusseldorf; Emil Richter, Dresden. At Montfavet with Braque and Picasso when war breaks out.

1914-18   Serves in Champaigne, Somme, Verdun, L'Aisne, Vosges. Executes a few pastels and drawings.

1915-16   Illustrates for *L'Elan*.

1916   Illustration for André Breton's *Mont-de-Piété*. 15-21 October. Exhibition at the Galerie Paul Guillaume, 16 avenue de Villiers, Paris. Preface by Guillaume Apollinaire. This catalogue contains the following poems: (1) G. Apollinaire, *Voyage*, dedicated to A.M.P.; (2) F. Divoire, *Ronde des Signes*; (3) P. Reverdy, *Nature Morte Portrait*; (4) Blaise Cendrars, *Bombay Express*; (5) Max Jacob, *La Messe du Visionnaire* (in verse and prose).

1918   Executes masks from shell cases. During the French occupation at Mayence, executes sets for *L'Annonce faite à Marie*, later performed by the Durec troupe in Scandinavia. Demobilized.

1919   Paints *The Greek Girl; Portrait of Paul Guillaume*. Executes sets, costumes, and curtains for Diaghileff's ballet *La Boutique Fantasque*, first performed in London at the Alhambra Theatre in 1919. Meets Clive Bell. His designs published by J. Miles and Co., London. Illustrates René

Dalize, *Ballade de Pauvre Macchabé mal enterré* (F. Bernouard). Lithograph for Vlaminck's *A la santé du Corps*. Modigliani draws portraits of Derain and Madame Derain.

1920   Executes decorations for the apartment of Norwegian dealer Halvorsen in Paris. Works at Cahors. Begins series of portraits and nudes. Kahnweiler returns to Paris and buys his work until 1922. Derain's portrait drawn by Picasso. Illustrations for André Salmon's *Le Calumet*, and for *Le Nez de Cléopatre* (Simon). Exhibition of drawings for Dalize's *Ballade* at La Belle Edition, Paris.

1921   Visits Rome: paints series of landscapes at Castel Gandolfo. Works in Le Midi at Sanary and Le Ciotat; with Kisling at Sanary in the summer; paints Kisling's portrait. Paints *Portrait of Georges Gabory*. Illustrations for P. Reverdy's *Etoiles Peintes*. (Le Sagittaire.)

1922   Works at Sanary, Les Lecques and at Saint Cyr-sur-Mer. September: exhibits at the Svensk-Franska Konstgalleriet, Stockholm; October, exhibits at Flechtheim, Berlin; Kahnweiler, Frankfurt-am-Main; December-January 1923 at Moderne Galerie (Thannhauser), Munich; Brummer, 43 East 57th Street, New York (Preface by J. Brummer). Kahnweiler ceases to buy his work. Illustrates Gabory's *La Cassette de Plomb* (Bernouard).

1923   Paints *Portrait of Madame Hessling*, the wife of Jean Renoir, in exchange for four small paintings by Renoir. Paul Guillaume becomes his dealer. Exhibits: Flechtheim, Berlin. Visits Utrillo at St Bernard; Utrillo gives him a gouache of Dr Marteau's clinic. Buys his first painting by Corot: the *Portrait of Mlle Puyparlier*.

1924   Paints *Pierrot and Harlequin* (Fig. 61) and *The Kitchen Table* (Fig. 62). Designs *décor* for *Gigues* (Soirées de Paris). Paints flowers and nudes.

1925   Paints *Portrait of Vincent Muselli* (Fig. 59), Paris. Paintings and drawings of dancers. Works at Nice, Les Lecques.

1926   Illustrates G. Coquiot's *En suivant la Seine* (André Delpeuch). Designs *décor* for ballet *Jack in the Box*, music by Erik Satie, which was commissioned by Comte Etienne de Beaumont and later taken over by the Russian Ballet.

1927   Exhibits: Flechtheim, Dusseldorf.

1928   Paints *The Large Nude* (Fig. 65). *Dead Game* (Fig. 63) wins the Carnegie Prize. Exhibits: March, The Lefevre Gallery, London.

1929   Paints *Portrait of Madame Paul Guillaume*. Exhibits: April, Flechtheim, Berlin; Kahnweiler,

Frankfurt-am-Main; June, Paul Guillaume, Paris; November, Flechtheim, Dusseldorf. Illustrates V. Muselli's *Les Travaux et les Jeux* (Pouterman).

1930 Paints important series of landscapes at Saint Maximin, Var and at Bandol. Exhibits: April, Knoedler, New York (Preface by Etienne Bignou); December-January 1931, Cincinnati Art Museum. About this period exchanges Negro objects for Graeco-Roman and Egypto-Roman portraits.

1931 Exhibits: 'New Paintings by Derain', The Lefevre Gallery, London; March, 'Paysages de Provence', Marie Harriman Gallery, New York; May, Galerie Schwarzenberg, Brussels.

1932 Illustrates Ovid's *Les Héroïdes*. Designs sets for *La Concurrence*, music by Georges Auric, choreography by Balanchine, first performed by the Ballets Russes de Monte Carlo, 12 April, at Monte Carlo. Works at St Rémy.

1933 Paints *The Two Men*. Designs sets for *Fastes*, music by Henri Sauguet, choreography by Balanchine, first performed on 10 June at the Théâtre des Champs Elysées, and for *Songes*, music by Darius Milhaud, choreography by Balanchine, first performed on 7 June at the Théâtre des Champs Elysées, Paris. Works at St Rémy. Exhibits: February-March, Durand Ruel, New York (Preface by Waldemar George); May, *décor* and ballet designs at Quatre-Chemins, Paris; November-December, 'Recent Paintings 1930-33', Arthur Tooth and Sons Ltd., London. Sells part of his collection of Negro art.

1934 Paints at Gravelines, Dunkirk and St Rémy. Illustrates Petronius' *Le Satyricon* for Ambroise Vollard and A. Artaud's *d'Héliogabale* (Denoël and Steele).

1935 Moves to Chambourcy, which remains his country home until his death. Paints landscapes in the Ile de France. Illustrates *Voyage en Grèce été*, 1935, and R. Wilnes, *Réflexions d'une innocente* (Véga). Exhibits: February, Svensk-Franska Konstgalleriet, Stockholm; May, Renou et Colle, Paris; June, Kunsthalle, Berne (large retrospective), 'New Pictures by Derain', T. Agnew and Sons, London.

1936 Paints at Douarnenez, St Rémy, Portofino. Designs set for *L'Epreuve d'Amour*, music by Mozart, choreography by Fokine, first performed by the Ballets Russe de Monte Carlo on 4 April at Monte Carlo. Exhibits: J. Brummer, New York.

1937 Retrospective Exhibition at the Salon des Indépendants, Petit Palais, Paris. Exhibits: Messrs Reid and Lefevre, London. Visits London.

1938 Paints *Chantier de Bateaux*. Many portraits of his niece Geneviève. Starts *The Painter with his Family* (Fig. 75). Illustrates Oscar Wilde's *Salomé* (The Limited Editions Club, New York); Ovid's *Les Héroïdes* (Société les Cents Unes, Paris).

1939 Exhibits: February-March, Lilienfeld Galleries, New York.

1940 Paints at Vichy.

1941 Paints on the Loire. Exhibits: April-May, 'Paintings from 1938 and After', Pierre Matisse Gallery, New York. Studio in the Rue de Varenne, Paris.

1943 Paints landscapes at Donnemarie. Illustrates Rabelais' *Pantagruel* (Skira). Visits Germany.

1944 At Chambourcy.

1945 Paints *The Hunt*.

1946 Paints *Amiens* (Fig. 84).

1947 Paints *The Virgin*. Exhibition: 'Chatou' at Galerie Bing, Paris. Illustrates Héron de Villefosse's *L'Eloge de Pierreries*. Designs set for *Mam'zelle Angot*, a ballet with music after Charles Lecocq, orchestrated by Gordon Jacob, performed by the Sadlers Wells Ballet, at Covent Garden. November, Derain visits London.

1948 Designs sets for *Le Diable l'emporte*, with music derived from eighteenth-century popular airs, chosen by Roland Petit and orchestrated by Manuel Rosenthal, with argument, *décors* and costumes by Derain, first performed 1 June at Théâtre Marigny, Paris, by Ballets Roland Petit.

1949 March: Exhibition 'Hommage à Derain' at Galerie de Berri, Paris (Preface by W. George).

1950 Paints landscapes at Noirmoutier and Dieppe. Illustrates La Fontaine, *Contes et Nouvelles* (Foquet et Bandier); Saint Exupéry, *Œuvres* (Gallimard).

1951 July, designs sets for Mozart's *Il Seraglio* for the Festival at Aix en Provence.

1953 July, designs sets for Rossini's *The Barber of Seville* for the Festival at Aix en Provence.

1954 Derain dies on 8 September. Memorial Exhibition, Musée d'Art Moderne, Paris (Preface by Jean Cassou). Derain exhibition at XXVII Biennale.

1955 May-September. 'Cinquante Tableaux Importants d'André Derain' at the Galerie Charpentier, Paris (Preface by Georges Hilaire). March. Sales of his collections at the Galerie Charpentier and at the Hôtel Drouot. July exhibition at the Galerie Jeanne Castel (Preface Georges Hilaire). September-October, Galerie Paul Vallotton, Lausanne. October-November, exhibition at Galerie Motte, Lausanne (Preface by V. Photiades).

'Retrospective Derain' III Biennale, São Paulo, Brazil. 'Derain', Salon d' Automne, Paris (Preface by Dunoyer de Segonzac).

1957 March, exhibition, 'Drawings by Derain', at Galerie Maeght, Paris. Exhibition at Wildenstein Gallery, London.

1958 Autumn, 'Derain' at Galerie Maeght, Paris. 'Hommage à Derain', Salon d'Asnières. Prefaces by André Salmon and Florent Fels. (17 pictures from the Lévy collection.)

1959 July-October 'André Derain', Museé de l'Athénée, Geneva.

Derain was also represented in the following exhibitions devoted to Fauvism: 1927, Galerie Bing, Paris; 1934, Galerie des Beaux Arts, Paris; 1935, Petit Palais, Grenoble; 1941, Marie Harriman Gallery, New York; 1942, Galerie de France, Paris; 1950, Kunsthalle, Berne: The Biennale, Venice; Sidney Janis Gallery, New York; 1951, Musée d'Art Moderne, Paris; 1952, Museum of Modern Art, New York; 1953, Institute of Arts, Minneapolis; Museum of Art, San Francisco; The Art Gallery, Toronto.

BIBLIOGRAPHY

Statements by Derain

Interview given to *Le Matin* 6 April 1920 on the occasion of the fourth centenary of Raphael's death, summarized by André Salmon in *Propos d'Atelier*, 1938, pp. 148-53.

Interview with René Crevel, published in *Commune*, No. 21, and reprinted in *De la Palette à l'Ecritoire*, ed. André Lhote, 1946, pp. 393-5.

'Idées d'un Peintre': interview with André Breton, published in *Les Pas Perdus*, 1924, pp. 105-12. A German translation appeared in K. Westheim, *Künstlerbekenntnisse* (n.d.), pp. 151-4.

Florent Fels, 'Derain' in *Propos d'Artistes*, 1925, pp. 37-43.

Statement on 'Fauvism', given to Georges Duthuit in 'Le Fauvisme', in *Cahiers d'Art*, 1929 (iv), p. 268.

'Quand les Fauves, Quelque Souvenirs . . .', in *Comoedia*, 20 June 1942.

Gotthard Jedlicka, 'Begegnung mit André Derain' in *Begegnungen mit Künstlern der Gegenwart*, 1945, pp. 112-132.

Note on Chatou published in the catalogue of the exhibition *Chatou* at the Galerie Bing, Paris, 1947.

Extracts from an unpublished manuscript *De l'Art de Peindre*, printed in the catalogue of the Memorial Exhibition at the Musée d'Art Moderne, Paris, 1954.

Lettres à Vlaminck, ed. M. Vlaminck, 1955.

Interview with Denys Sutton in 'André Derain: Art as Fate', published in *Encounter*, October 1955, pp. 68-72.

'Propos de Derain', collected by Madame Pierre Lévy in *Du*, October 1956, pp. 30-39, and in *Prisme des Arts*, No. 6, November 1956, pp. 2-6.

Extract from a *Cahier d'André Derain*, published in *Derrière le Miroir* (issued by the Galerie Maeght), 1957.

Select List of Books and Articles

Jean Adhémar, *L'Œuvre gravé de Derain*. Catalogue of an exhibition held at the Bibliothèque Nationale, Paris, 1955.

Ronald Alley, *Tate Gallery. Foreign Paintings, Drawings and Sculpture*, 1959.

Guillaume Apollinaire, *Les Peintres Cubistes*, 1913 (an English translation was issued in New York in 1944).

Alfred Barr, *Picasso. Fifty Years of his Art*. 1946.

Alfred Barr, *Matisse. His Art and his Public*. 1951.

Adolphe Basler, *Derain*. 1929.

Adolphe Basler, *Derain*. Album Druet, xxi, 1929.

Cyril W. Beaumont, *Complete Book of Ballets*. 1949.

Clive Bell, 'The Authority of M. Derain' in *Since Cézanne*. 1922.

Clive Bell, 'Derain' in *Formes*. February 1930.

Clive Bell, *Old Friends*. 1956.

Francis Carco, *L'Ami du Peintre*. 1944.

Carlo Carrà, *Derain*. 1921. (English edition, 1924.)

Jean Cassou, 'Derain' in *Cahiers d'Art*, October, 1926, pp. 189-197.

Douglas Cooper, 'Derain Exhibition at the Musée d'Art Moderne' in *The Burlington Magazine*, xcvII, February 1955.

Pierre Courthion, *Panorama de la Peinture Française Contemporaine*. 1927.

Henry Daniel (pseudonym for D. H. Kahnweiler), *André Derain*. 1920 (a Dutch edition was issued in 1924).

Henry Daniel, *Der Weg zum Kubismus*. 1920 (an English translation was issued in New York in 1951, London 1956).

Bernard Dorival, *Les Etapes de la Peinture Française*. 1944, vol. II.

Georges Duthuit, 'Le Fauvisme' in *Cahiers d'Art*. 1929, 1930, 1931.

Georges Duthuit, *Les Fauves*. 1949 (an English translation was issued in New York in 1950).

Carl Einstein, *Die Kunst des XX Jahrhunderts*. 1926 and 1931.

Elie Faure, *Derain*. 1923.

Waldemar George, 'Derain' in *Histoire de l'Art Contemporain*, ed. René Huyghe. 1933.

Waldemar George, 'Derain peintre de l'intemperel' in *Prisme des Arts*, No. 13, 1957, pp. 24-27.

Alberto Giacometti, 'Derain' in *Derrière le Miroir*, Galerie Maeght, 1957.

Robert Goldwater, *Primitivism in Modern Painting*. 1938.

Werner Haftmann, *Malerei im 20 Jahrhundert*. 1948.

Max Jacob, *Correspondance* (1876-1921), ed. François Garnier. 1953.

Daniel Henry Kahnweiler, *Juan Gris, His Life and Work* (translated by Douglas Cooper). 1947.

Jean Leymarie, *André Derain ou le retour à l'Ontologie* 1948.

Jean Leymarie, *Fauvism*. 1959.

Pierre Mornand, 'André Derain', in *Vingt-deux Artistes du Livre*, 1948, pp. 131-144.

Joseph Emile Muller, *Le Fauvisme*. 1956.

Benedict Nicolson, 'Post-Impressionism and Roger Fry' in *The Burlington Magazine*, XCIII, January 1951.

Fernande Olivier, *Picasso et Ses Amis*. 1933.

Roland Penrose, *Picasso*. 1958.

Maurice Raynal, 'André Derain' in *L'Esprit Nouveau*. 1921.

Maurice Raynal, *Anthologie de la Peinture Française de 1906 à Nos Jours*. 1927.

John Rewald, *Les Fauves*. 1952.

André Salmon, *La Jeune Peinture Française*. 1912.

André Salmon, *L'Art Vivant*. 1920.

André Salmon, *André Derain*. 1924.

André Salmon, *André Derain*. 1929.

André Salmon, *Propos d'Atelier*. 1938.

André Salmon, *Souvenirs sans Fin*, 2 vols. 1956.

Marc Sandoz, *Eloge de Derain*, 1958.

Gertrude Stein, *The Autobiography of Alice B. Toklas*. 1933.

Denys Sutton, 'The Fauves' in *The Burlington Magazine*, XCII, September 1950.

Denys Sutton, 'André Derain: Art as Fate', in *Encounter*. October 1955, pp. 68-72.

Denys Sutton, *André Derain. Catalogue of Loan Exhibition* at the Wildenstein Gallery, London. 1957.

[David Sylvester], 'André Derain: the Decline of a Reputation' in *The Times*, 13 May 1955.

Dimitris Tselos, 'Derain and Medievalism' in *Parnassus*. March 1938, pp. 7-10.

M. Valotaire, 'Derain' in *Art and Design*, IV, 1927, pp. 70-75.

Malcolm Vaughan, *Derain*. 1941.

Maurice Vlaminck, *Tournant Dangereux*. 1929.

Maurice Vlaminck, *Portraits avant Décès*. 1943.

R. H. Wilenski, 'André Derain. An Austere Romantic' in *Apollo*. 1928.

Christian Zervos, *Histoire de l'Art Contemporain*. 1938.

Pour ou Contre Derain: Les Chroniques du Jour. January 1931. (Special number devoted to Derain with contributions by G. Rouault, P. Courthion, A. Farcy, Waldemar George, André Salmon, M. G. Michel, R. Brielle, etc.)

History of Modern Painting, M. Raynal, A. Rudlinger, J. Bolliger, J. Lassaigne, vol. II. 1950.

A comprehensive bibliography of books and articles on Derain is given in A. Vollmer, *Allgemeines Lexikon der Bildenden Künstler des XX. Jahrhunderts*. 1953.

NOTES ON THE ILLUSTRATIONS

As far as possible I have attempted to supply the relevant information concerning
the works reproduced in this volume. However, in some cases it
has not proved possible to give the measurements.

Abbreviations:

'Memorial', Paris, 1954-1955, refers to the catalogue of the exhibition of Derain's work held
at the Museé National d'Art Moderne, Paris, 1954-1955. Preface by Jean Cassou, text by
Madame Vienne.

'Derain', Charpentier, Paris, refers to the exhibition held at the Galerie Charpentier, 1955.
Preface by Georges Hilaire.

'Derain', London, 1957, refers to the exhibition held at the Wildenstein Gallery, London,
1957, organized and catalogued by Denys Sutton.

'Derain', Geneva, 1959, refers to the exhibition held at the Musée de L'Athéneé, Geneva,
1959.

1. SELF-PORTRAIT (*Autoportrait*). Canvas. Private
Collection, Paris.
Collection: Ambroise Vollard, Paris.
According to Madame Alice Derain, this was
painted about 1895-1899. The summary treatment
of the jug with brushes is a characteristic element
of Derain's style which was employed throughout
his career.

2. THE ROAD TO CARRIÈRES (*La Route de Car-
rières*). Canvas, 18 $\frac{18}{16}$ × 25 $\frac{3}{16}$ in. (48 × 64 cm.). Private
Collection, Paris.
Signed and dated lower left 1899.
Exhibited: 'Memorial', Paris, 1954-1955 (1).
The earliest dated work so far recorded. Painted on
the outskirts of Paris, it suggests that Derain was
already aware of Gauguin and Cézanne. Another
picture — *A Suburban Street* — is reproduced by
André Salmon, *Derain*, 1929, p. 12, as being from
the same year.

3. THE FUNERAL (*L'Enterrement*). Canvas. Madame
Matisse, Paris.
According to Madame Alice Derain, this sparkling
canvas, which indicates the influence of Manet on
the artist, was painted about 1899. It represents the
street at Chatou in which the painter's family lived.
Another painting of Chatou, *A Corner at Chatou*,
stated to be of 1900, was exhibited at the Galerie
Bing, 1947, and reproduced in an album, *Chatou*,
issued on this occasion.

4. THE BALL AT SURESNES (*Le Bal à Suresnes*).
Canvas, 69 $\frac{5}{16}$ × 66 $\frac{3}{16}$ in. (176 × 168 cm.). City Art
Museum, Saint Louis, U.S.A.
Signed and dated 1903 lower right.
Collection: Carroll Carstairs, New York.
Exhibited: 'Derain', Brummer Gallery, New York,
1936(42); Wadsworth Atheneum, Hartford, Conn.,
1943; 'Memorial', Paris, 1954-1955 (3).
Literature: Malcolm Vaughan, *Derain*, 1941, frontis-
piece in colour; Jacquelin Ambler, 'At the Suresnes
Ball' in *Bulletin: City Art Museum*, St. Louis, xxx,
August 1945, pp. 26-28 (repr.).
Painted in 1903 during the period when Derain
was with the 155th Infantry Regiment at Commercy. It is not known if the picture was actually
executed while he was with the regiment or while
on leave. The suggestion that the artist himself is
represented in the picture is untenable.

5. THE DANCER (*La Danseuse*). Canvas, 39 $\frac{3}{8}$ × 31 $\frac{7}{8}$
in. (100 × 81 cm.). Statens Museum, Copenhagen.
Collections: Galerie Kahnweiler, Paris (No. 2031);
D. H. Kahnweiler sale, Paris, 7-8 May 1923 (171);
bt. J. Rump.
Exhibited: Grønningens Udstilling, Copenhagen,
1942 (10).
Literature: Carlo Carrà, *Derain*, 1921, Fig. 21; Leo
Swane in *Kunstmuseet Aarskrift*, xvi-xviii, 1929-1931,
p. 76; E. Zahle, *Fransk Maleri efter* 1900, 1938,
p. 15, plate 17; Jesper Engelstoft, *Verdens billedkunst
efter* 1800, 1955, plate 56; Werner Haftmann,

Malerei im 20 Jahrhundert, 1955, p. 56, plate 10; *Statens Museum, Moderne Udenlansk Kunst*, ed. Hanne Finsen, 1958, No. R.141 (repr.); Jean Leymarie, *Fauvisme*, 1959, p. 124 (in colour).

Painted in 1906. The same model also sat to Vlaminck; cf. *La Danseuse du rat mort*, repr. in J. Leymarie, op. cit., p. 125. This is one of Derain's first paintings of women.

6. THE BEDROOM (*La Chambre à coucher*). Canvas, 13 × 16 in. (33 × 40 cm.). Mrs. Gerald Corcoran, London.

Signed lower right.

Collection: Messrs. Reid and Lefevre, London.

Exhibited: 'French Painting of the XIXth and XXth Centuries', Lefevre Gallery, London, 1954 (7 repr.); 'XXth Century French Masters', Lefevre Gallery, London, 1958 (4, repr.).

This would seem to be datable to about 1900-1901 and was presumably painted at Chatou. A related composition, depicting a girl seated in the same room which is of the same size, was once with Messrs. Reid and Lefevre, London; see 'School of Paris', Lefevre Gallery, London, 1951 (7). A painting of a *Boat on the River* (Mr. and Mrs. Lazarus Phillips, Montreal) appears to date from the same period: see 'XXth Century French Painters,' Lefevre Gallery, London, 1958 (5, repr.).

7. STILL LIFE (*Nature morte*). Canvas, 40 × 41 $\frac{13}{16}$ in. (115 × 164 cm.). Madame Charles Baron, Paris.

Signed and dated 1904 lower right.

Exhibited: 'Memorial', Paris, 1954-1955 (10).

One of Derain's most important early paintings in which his interest in Cézanne and Gauguin is already evident.

8. SNOWSCAPE AT CHATOU (*Paysage de neige à Chatou*). Cardboard laid down on canvas, 31 $\frac{7}{8}$ × 24 in. (81 × 61 cm.). Comte Armand Doria, Paris.

Signed lower left.

Collections: Ambroise Vollard, from whom bought by Comte Doria, the father of the present owner, on 27 July 1912 for 200 francs.

Exhibited: 'Memorial', Paris, 1954-1955 (*hors catalogue*); 'Derain', III Biennale, São Paulo, Brazil, 1955 (2); 'Derain', London, 1957 (4, repr.).

Literature: Connaissance des Arts, No. 2, 15 April 1953, pp. 10-11, repr.

This view of Chatou dates from Derain's early Fauve period, c.1904. It bears certain stylistic resemblances to his paintings of Le Pecq from that date, cf. Fig. 9. It presumably formed part of the

group of pictures which Ambroise Vollard, the dealer, acquired from the artist in February 1905.

9. THE BRIDGE AT LE PECQ (*Le Pont du Le Pecq*). Canvas, 31 $\frac{7}{8}$ × 45 $\frac{5}{8}$ in. (81 × 116 cm.). Monsieur Roger Gros, Paris.

Signed lower right and inscribed *Le Pecq*.

Collections: Galerie Kahnweiler, Paris (No. 2164); D. H. Kahnweiler sale, Hôtel Drouot, Paris, 7-8 May 1923 (175, as *Le Pont de Chatou*); Marc François.

Exhibited: 'Les Fauves', Berne, 1947 (17); Musée de Lyon, 1949 (29); 'Derain', XXV Biennale, Venice, 1950 (8); 'Memorial', Paris, 1954-1955 (7); 'Derain', London, 1957 (5).

Literature: Daniel Henry, *Derain*, 1920, plate I; Edouard-Joseph, *Dictionnaire Biographique des Artistes Contemporains*, 1930, repr., p. 392; Georges Duthuit, *Les Fauves*, 1949, p. 44, repr.

Painted in 1904.

10. VINEYARDS IN SPRING (*Les Vignes au Printemps*). Canvas, 35 $\frac{1}{16}$ × 44 $\frac{7}{8}$ in. (89,5 × 116,5 cm.). Kunstmuseum, Basle.

Signed lower right.

Exhibited: 'Les Fauves', Kunsthalle, Berne, 1947 (21); 'Fauves', XXV Biennale, Venice, 1950 (10, as 1906).

Literature: Basle Museum Catalogue, 1946, 145 (Inv. No. 1472); Jean Leymarie, *André Derain*, 1948, Fig. 2 (in colour); Georges Duthuit, *Les Fauves*, 1949, repr., p. 133; Florent Fels, *L'Art Vivant*, I, 1950, p. 175.

This canvas, which suggests the influence of Van Gogh, was painted about 1906.

11. COLLIOURE. Canvas, 28 $\frac{3}{8}$ × 35 $\frac{7}{8}$ in. (72 × 91 cm.). Monsieur Pierre Lévy, Troyes.

Signed lower left.

Exhibited: 'Les Fauves', Berne, 1950 (15) as *Petit Port*; 'Autour de 1900', Galerie Charpentier, Paris, 1951 (70); 'Le Fauvisme', Musée d'Art Moderne, Paris, 1951 (41, repr. p. 18); 'Les Fauves', Museum of Modern Art, New York, 1952-3 (36); id. at Museum of Art, Minneapolis, 1953; id. at San Francisco Museum, 1953; id. at Art Gallery, Toronto, 1953; 'Derain', Galerie Charpentier, Paris, 1955 (7, repr.); 'André Derain', Galerie Motte, Geneva (2); 'Derain', London, 1957 (7, as *L'Estaque*).

Literature: John Rewald, *Les Fauves*, 1952, p. 23, repr. as 'Collioure, the White Horse, 1907'; J. E.

Muller, *Le Fauvisme*, Paris, 1956, p. 33, repr. as *Le Port de Collioure*.

Painted at Collioure in 1905 while the artist was staying there with Matisse and Madame Matisse. A not dissimilar composition is in a Swiss private collection, see Georges Duthuit, *Les Fauves*, 1949, repr. in colour, p. 129.

12. THE HOUSES OF PARLIAMENT (*Le Big Ben*). Canvas, 31⅛ × 38⅝ in. (79 × 98 cm.). Monsieur Pierre Lévy, Troyes.
Collection: Ambroise Vollard, Paris.
Exhibited: 'Derain', Galerie Charpentier, Paris, 1955 (4, repr.); 'Derain', Wildenstein, London, 1957 (9).
Literature: Le Nouveau Femina, November 1956; J. E. Muller, *Le Fauvisme*, 1956, p. 30, in colour; *Du*, October 1956, repr. p. 32.
Probably executed in 1905 on Derain's first visit to London at the same time as the *Houses of Parliament* in the Musée de l'Annonciade, St. Tropez (repr. in J. E. Muller, op. cit., p. 31 in colour). The style of both pictures indicates that the artist had studied Signac and the Neo-Impressionists; the idea of painting a London series was derived from Monet. It may also be compared with *Reflections on Water* in the Musée de l'Annonciade, St. Tropez (repr. Jean Leymarie, *Fauvism*, 1959, p. 68) and *Old Waterloo Bridge*, formerly with Messrs. Reid and Lefevre, London.

13. HYDE PARK. Canvas, 26 × 31 in. (66 × 99 cm.). Monsieur Pierre Lévy, Troyes.
Signed lower right.
Collection: Ambroise Vollard, Paris; Messrs. Reid and Lefevre, London.
Exhibited: 'The Thames, 1907', Reid and Lefevre, 1937 (3); 'Les Fauves', Kunsthalle, Berne, 1950; 'Fauves', XXV Biennale, Venice, 1950 (15); 'Autour de 1900', Galerie Charpentier, Paris, 1950 (69, repr.); 'Le Fauvisme', Paris, 1951 (43); 'The Fauves', Museum of Modern Art, New York, 1952-1953; id. Minneapolis; Institute of Arts, San Francisco, 1953; Art Gallery, Toronto, 1953; Musée Granet, Aix-en-Provence, 1954 (4, repr.); 'Derain', Galerie Charpentier, Paris, 1955 (6); 'Derain', Galerie Motte, Geneva, 1955 (1, repr.); 'Europa 1907', Stedelijk Museum, Amsterdam, 1957 (22, repr.).
Literature: Gaston Diehl, *Les Fauves*, 1943, plate 3; Georges Besson, 1900-1940 *Couleurs des Maîtres*, plate 11; John Rewald, *The Fauves*, 1952, p. 45; *Art News Annual*, 1953, repr. p. 102; J. E. Muller, *Le Fauvisme*, 1956, repr. p. 62; *Les Arts*, 29 October-4 November 1958, repr. p. 16.

Painted in London, probably in 1906. It suggests Derain's connection with Gauguin and Art Nouveau.

14. THE GOLDEN AGE (*L'Age d'Or*). Canvas, 74¼ × 69½ in. (190 × 180 cm.). Mr. Walter P. Chrysler Jnr., New York.
Collections: Galerie Kleinman, Paris; Robert Lebel, Paris.
Exhibited: 'Les Fauves', Kunsthalle, Berne, 1950 (12, as 1905); 'Fauves', XXV Biennale, Venice, 1950 (9, as 1904-1905); 'Le Fauvisme', Musée d'Art Moderne, Paris, 1951 (39); 'Walter P. Chrysler Jnr. collection', Portland Art Museum, Oregon, 1956 (91, repr.).
Literature: Denys Sutton, 'The Fauves', *Burlington Magazine*, XCII, September 1950, p. 264, Fig. 18; Jean Leymarie, *Fauvisme*, 1959, p. 81.
According to Jean Leymarie (op. cit. p. 81) this was painted in the summer of 1905 at Collioure. It clearly demonstrates Derain's dependence on the pointillist principles, and the iconography of the picture, derived from Ovid's *Metamorphoses*, indicates the interest in classical themes shown by certain Fauve painters at this time.

15. THE DANCE (*La Danse*). Canvas, 73 × 90 in. (185,4 × 228,4 cm.). Messrs. Knoedler and Co., New York.
Collection: Léon Pédron; Pédron sale, Paris, Hôtel Drouot, 2 June 1926 (12, repr. as *Fresque Hindoue*).
Exhibited: 'Memorial', Paris, 1954-1955 (19, repr. plate V as 1909).
Literature: Vogue (Paris edition), December 1954 - January 1955, p. 93 (in colour, as 1908); *Burlington Magazine*, advertisement supplement, c, December 1958, plate XXXII (as 1909).
It is probably safe to place this intriguing work with its echoes of Romanesque and Indian art and possibly of Bakst's decorations for the Russian Ballet, in the Fauvist period (1905-1906). It may be compared with two wood carvings, demonstrably influenced by Gauguin, which were once in the Paul Guillaume collection; see André Salmon, *André Derain*, 1929, pp. 24-25. Derain executed a number of watercolours on the theme of dancers in 1905-1906: For a water colour, 'The Dance', see Forbes Watson, *John Quinn Collection*, 1926, p. 50, and cf. also a watercolour of 'Bathers' in the possession of Mr. Jeremy Hutchinson, exhibited 'Derain', London, 1957 (13).

16. TURNING ROAD, L'ESTAQUE (*La route tournant, L'Estaque*). Canvas, 51 × 76¾ in. (130 × 195 cm.). Monsieur Pierre Blay, Paris.
Exhibited: 'Les Fauves', Museum of Modern Art, New York, 30 repr., p. 20, 1952-1953; The Minneapolis Institute of Arts; Museum of Art, San Francisco; Art Gallery, Toronto, 1953; 'Derain', Charpentier, Paris, 1955 (8, repr.).
Literature: John Rewald, *Les Fauves*, 1952, repr., p. 20.
Painted in 1905. It suggests Derain's interest in Gauguin.

17. LANDSCAPE AT CASSIS (*Paysage à Cassis*). Canvas, 28½ × 36¼ in. (73 × 92 cm.). Private Collection, Paris.
Signed and dated lower right 1906.
Exhibited: 'Memorial', Paris, 1954-1955 (14).
One of Derain's few dated canvases, it reveals his interest in the simplification of forms at a relatively early date: it may even suggest that he was aware of Javlensky's work which he could have seen at this period.

18. LANDSCAPE AT CASSIS (*Paysage à Cassis*). Canvas, 21½ × 25¼ in. (54 × 64 cm.). Monsieur Pierre Lévy, Troyes.
Signed lower right.
Collection: Galerie Kahnweiler, Paris (No. 2059).
Exhibited: 'Memorial', Paris, 1954-1955 (17); 'Derain', London, 1957 (15 repr.); 'Les Soirées de Paris', Knoedler, Paris, 1958 (10, repr., as 1910); 'Derain', Salon d'Asnières, October 1958 (4, repr.). 'Derain', Geneva, 1959 (15, repr.).
Painted at Cassis in 1907, it suggests Derain's interest in simplification at this period and may be compared with No. 17.

19. NUDE FIGURES (*Nus*). Canvas, 17⅞ × 14 in. (45,5 × 35,5 cm.). Private Collection, Paris.
Collections: Galerie Kahnweiler, Paris (No. 2184); Willy Streit, Hamburg; Messrs. Matthiesen, London; Galerie Romanet, Paris.
Exhibited: Hamburg, 1930 (35).
Literature: Daniel Henry, 'André Derain', *Cicerone*, XII (1920), p. 316; Daniel Henry, *Derain*, 1920, plate 6 (as 1907); Robert Goldwater, *Primitivism in Modern Painting*, 1938, plate VII (as 1908), p. 77.
Painted in 1907. One of Derain's few surviving nude studies from this period, of which the majority were destroyed by the artist himself. Others include *The Toilet* (repr. Daniel Henry, op. cit., plate 9), *The Bathers* (Müller collection, Solothurn, repr.

Daniel Henry, op. cit. plate 3), *Nudes* (repr. R. Goldwater, op. cit. plate VII), and *Nudes* (sold, Paris, Hôtel Drouot, 5-6 June 1951) (41, repr. plate X).

20. THE BATHERS (*Les Baigneurs*). Canvas, 70¼ × 98½ in. (180 × 225 cm.). Present whereabouts unknown.
Signed lower right.
Collections: Galerie Kahnweiler, Paris (No. 2121); Anon. sale, Paris, Hôtel Drouot, 9 June 1928 (40, repr.).
Exhibited: 'Internationale Kunstausstellung', Dresden, 1926.
Literature: André Salmon, *Derain*, 1923 repr. p. 19; Carlo Carrà, *Derain*, 1924, Fig. 27; Will Grohmann, 'Die Kunst der Gegenwart', in *Cicerone*, XVIII, June 1926, p. 329 repr.; Carl Einstein, *Die Kunst des 20 Jahrhunderts*, 1926, p. 37, repr. p. 199.
Painted in 1908. One of the few figure pieces by Derain to have survived from this period. For a note on his painting of nudes at this time, see No. 19.

21. THE RED HOUSE (*La Maison Rouge*). Canvas, 36½ × 28¾ in. (92 × 71 cm.). E. Teltsch, Esq., London.
Signed lower right.
Collection: Galerie Kahnweiler, Paris (No. 2016); D. H. Kahnweiler sale, Hôtel Drouot, Paris, 17-18 November 1921 (66); Mrs. M. M. Richardson, sold, Sotheby's, 28 November 1956 (109); The Leicester Galleries, London.
One of a series painted at Montreuil-sur-Mer in 1909: cf. Daniel Henry, *Derain*, 1920, plate 11.

22. THE OLD BRIDGE AT CAGNES (*Le Vieux Pont à Cagnes*). Canvas, 31⅞ × 39½ in. (81,3 × 99,6 cm.). National Gallery of Art, Washington, D.C. (Chester Dale collection).
Signed lower right.
Collections: Galerie Kahnweiler, Paris (No. 2003); Jean Laroche, Deauville; 'Villa Sauge Pourprée', sale, Paris, Hôtel Drouot, 8 December 1929 (43, repr.).
Exhibited: Sonderbund, Cologne, 1912; Stockholm, 1924 (434); 'Painting in Paris', Museum of Modern Art, New York, 1930 (20); 'Derain-Vlaminck', Museum of French Art, New York, 1922 (13).
Literature: Daniel Henry, 'André Derain' in *Cicerone*, XII, 1920, p. 321; Daniel Henry, *Derain*, 1920, plate 13; André Salmon, *Derain*, 1923, repr. p. 23; J. Gordon, *Modern French Painters*, 1923, repr. facing p. 124 (in colour); A. Ozenfant and Jeannerat, *La Peinture Moderne*, 1925, repr. p. 91; *Pour ou Contre Derain* (*Les Chroniques du Jour*), 1931, plate 2; C.

Zervos, *Histoire de l'Art Contemporain*, 1938, repr. p. 174; Malcolm Vaughan, *Derain*, 1941, repr. p. 11 (in colour); *Twentieth Century French Paintings from the Chester Dale Collection*, 1952, p. 18 repr.
Painted in 1910. A watercolour sketch, made probably from nature and without the figure on the right, is in the Tate Gallery, London; see R. Alley, *Tate Gallery, The Foreign Paintings, Drawings, Sculpture*, 1959, p. 65.
Derain painted a number of 'cubistic' views of Cagnes. cf: for instance, those in the Folkwang Museum, Essen, the Wallraf-Richartz Museum, Cologne, and Basel Museum (Rudolf Staechelin Collection).

23. CARRIÈRES-SAINT-DENIS. Canvas, 18½ × 21⅝ in. (46 × 55 cm.). Private collection, Paris.
Signed lower left.
Exhibited: 'Memorial', Paris, 1954-1955 (22).
Painted about 1909-1910. The present picture was described in the Memorial exhibition (22) as being of Chatou; however, according to Madame Alice Derain, it represents Carrières-Saint-Denis. A painting of Chatou from this date is in the collection of Dr. Willi Raeber, Basle: see 'Memorial', Paris, 1954-1955 (21).

24. CADAQUÈS. Canvas. 23¾ × 28¾ in. (60,5 × 73 cm.). Kunstmuseum, Basle.
Signed lower right.
Collections: Galerie Kahnweiler, Paris (No. 2001); Kramar; Rudolf Staechelin.
Exhibited: 'Derain', Kunsthalle, Berne, 1935 (16); Staechelin Memorial Exhibition, Kunstmuseum, Basle, 1956 (57, repr.)
Literature: Daniel Henry, *Derain*, 1920, plate 14; M. Raynal, 'André Derain', in *L'Esprit Nouveau*, 1921, repr. p. 886; André Salmon, *Derain*, 1923, repr. p. 25; C. Zervos, *Histoire de l'Art Contemporain*, 1938, repr. p. 174.
Painted in Cadaquès in Spain in 1910, while Derain was there with Picasso and Fernande. Another painting executed in Spain, but not apparently of Cadaquès, is in the possession of Mr. Eric Estorick, London; see 'Derain', London, 1957 (19); 'Memorial', Paris, 1954-1955, No. 25, repr. plate VI.

25. CAGNES. Canvas, 22 × 31 in. (60 × 81 cm.). Herr and Frau Rupf, Berne.
Signed on the reverse.
Collection: Galerie Kahnweiler, Paris (No. 2174), 1910, where bought by the present owner.
Exhibited: Internationale Kunstausstellung, Kunst-

haus, Zurich, 1925 (91); 'Derain', Kunsthalle, Berne, 1935 (17); 'Sammlung Rupf,' Kunsthalle, Basel, 1940 (7); 'Der Blaue Reiter, 1908-1914', Kunsthalle, Basel, 1950 (14); 'Europäische Kunst aus Berner Privatbesitz', Kunsthalle, Berne, 1953 (31); 'Sammlung Rupf,' Kunstmuseum, Berne, 1956 (22, repr.). 'Derain', Geneva, 1959 (16).
Literature: Jean Leymarie, *André Derain*, 1948, plate 4, in colour; M. Raynal, A. Rudlinger, J. Bolliger, J. Lassaigne, *Histoire de la Peinture Moderne*, 1950, repr. p. 65 in colour.
Painted in 1910. It indicates Derain's interest in Cézanne's water colours as well as his paintings.

26. STILL LIFE (*Nature morte*). Canvas, 36¼ × 28 in. (92 × 71 cm.). Private collection, Paris.
Signed lower right.
Collections: Galerie Kahnweiler, Paris (No. 2022); D. H. Kahnweiler sale, Paris, Hôtel Drouot, 13-14 June 1921 (46, repr.); Pellerin sale, Paris, Hôtel Drouot, 7 May 1926 (7, repr.).
Literature: W. George, 'André Derain', in *L'Amour de l'Art*, xiv, 1933, repr. fig. 195, p. 159; Jean Leymarie, *Derain*, 1948, plate 3 (in colour); M. Raynal, A. Rudlinger, H. Bolliger, J. Lassaigne, *Histoire de la Peinture Moderne*, 1950, repr. p. 64 (in colour).
Painted in 1910.

27. STILL LIFE (*Pommes et broc*). Canvas, 12 × 15⅞ in. (30,5 × 46,3 cm.). The Lady Pamela Berry, London.
Signed on lower right.
Collections: Galerie Kahnweiler, Paris; Mayor Gallery, London.
Exhibited: 'Derain', London, 1957 (20, repr.).
Painted in 1912.

28. THE ROAD AT CAMIERS (*La route de Camiers*). Canvas, 28½ × 36 in. (72,3 × 91,5 cm.). Present whereabouts unknown.
Collections: Galerie Kahnweiler, Paris (No. 2055); Otto Grautoff, Berlin; Dikran Kelekian; Kelekian sale, American Art Association, New York, 30-31 January 1923 (79, repr.).
Literature: Daniel Henry, *Derain*, 1920, plate 15; *Kunst und Künstler*, xix, 1920-1921, repr. p. 50; C. Zervos, *Histoire de l'Art Contemporain*, 1938, repr. p. 176.
Painted at Camiers in the Pas de Calais in 1911. A painting of the same motif, but without the figure, is in the collection of Dr. Willi Raeber, Basle.

29. THE CHURCH AT VERS (*L'Eglise de Vers*).
Canvas, 26 × 37 in. (66 × 94 cm.). E. A. Alport, Esq.,
Oxford.
Collections: Galerie Kahnweiler, Paris (No. 2042);
German private collection, 1929.
Exhibited: 'Derain', Alfred Flechtheim Galerie,
Berlin, 1929 (18); 'Apollinaire chez lui', Galerie
Apollinaire, London, 1947 (24); 'Derain', London,
1957 (22, repr.).
Literature: Daniel Henry, *Derain*, 1920, plate 19 (as
1912); E. Faure, *Derain*, 1923, plate 6 (as *Les Bords
du Lot*, 1913); Georg Bierman, 'Derain', in *Cicerone*,
xxi, 1929, repr. p. 231.
Painted in 1912. Another picture with a view of
the same church is reproduced by Carlo Carrà,
Derain, 1924, Fig. 19. The motif of a tree surmounted by a cross is also to be found in *Calvary*
(1912) in the Kunstmuseum, Basle, see Fig. 33.

30. INSIDE THE FOREST (*Dans la Forêt*). Canvas,
21⅞ × 25 3/16 in. (53 × 64 cm.). Mr. and Mrs. David
Meltzer, Toronto.
Signed lower right.
Collection: Madame Le Bec.
Exhibited: 'Derain', III Biennale, São Paulo, Brazil,
1955 (13).
Painted at Martigues about 1912. The technique
of this picture may be compared with *A Woodland
Scene* in the Soviet State Collection.

31. THE FOREST (*La Forêt*). Canvas, 15¾ × 18½ in.
(40 × 47 cm.). Herr and Frau Rupf, Berne.
Collections: Galerie Kahnweiler, Paris (No. 2009);
bought by the present owner in 1912.
Exhibited: 'Derain', Kunsthalle, Berne, 1935 (31);
'Sammlung Rupf,' Kunsthalle, Basel, 1940 (9);
Sammlung Rupf,' Kunstmuseum, Berne, 1956
(24, repr.). 'Derain', Geneva, 1959 (19).
Literature: André Salmon, *Derain*, 1929, plate II.
Painted at Martigues in 1912. The technique of
this picture is similar to a view of Camiers, repr. in
Carlo Carrà, *Derain*, 1924, Fig. 24.

32. THE BAGPIPER (*Le Joueur de cornemuse*). Canvas,
59 × 74 in. (150 × 188 cm.). Putnam D. McMillan
Land Company, U.S.A.
Collections: Galerie Kahnweiler, Paris (No. 2042);
John Quinn, New York; Valentine Gallery, New
York, bought J. T. Soby (1930); Curt Valentin,
New York.
Literature: Daniel Henry, *Derain*, 1920, plate 16;
André Salmon, *Derain*, 1923, repr. p. 27; Malcolm
Vaughan, *Derain*, 1941, pp. 55-56, repr. p. 25 in

colour; Forbes Watson, *John Quinn Collection*,
1926, repr. p. 45.
Painted in 1911. The theme was apparently suggested
to Derain by a chance encounter with a shepherd
playing his pipe at Camiers. According to M.
Vaughan (op. cit. p. 56), it was painted in the studio
from memory.

33. CALVARY (*Le Calvaire*). Canvas, 29 9/16 × 22⅝ in.
(65 × 57,5 cm.). Kunstmuseum, Basle.
Collections: Galerie Kahnweiler, Paris (No. 1055);
Matthiesen Galerie, Berlin; Dr. Karl Hagemann,
Frankfurt-am-Main; Folkwang Museum, Essen;
sold, T. Fischer, Lucerne, 30 June 1939 (32a, repr.).
Exhibited: 'Memorial', Paris, 1954-1955 (29, repr.
plate VII).
Literature: Jean Leymarie, *Derain*, 1948, plate 5 (in
colour), as 1913.
Painted at Vers in the Lot in 1912. Another painting
of the same year and representing the same hill
surmounted by a cross was with the Galerie Simon,
Paris; see M. Raynal, 'André Derain', in *L'Esprit
Nouveau*, 1921, repr. p. 897.

34. YOUNG GIRL (*La jeune fille*). Canvas, 25⅝ × 19⅝
in. (65 × 50 cm.). Pablo Picasso, Paris.
Collection: Galerie Kahnweiler, Paris (No. 2192).
Exhibited: 'Derain', Bibliothèque Nationale, Paris,
1955 (134).
Literature: Daniel Henry, 'André Derain' in *Cicerone*,
xii, 1920, repr. p. 329; Daniel Henry, *Derain*, 1920,
plate 27; André Salmon, *Derain*, 1923, repr. p. 41.
Painted in 1914. Two other pictures of young girls
also date from this period, one of which is in the
Hermitage; see C. Sterling, *Great French Paintings
in the Hermitage*, 1958, repr. fig. 58.

35. PORTRAIT OF ITURRINO. Canvas, 36¼ × 25⅞
in. (92 × 65 cm.). Monsieur N. Mazaraki, Vence,
Alpes-Maritimes.
Signed lower right.
Collections: Galerie Kahnweiler, Paris (No. 2220);
John Quinn, New York.
Exhibited: 'Memorial', Paris, 1954-1955 (43, repr.
plate XI as 1922); 'Derain', Galerie Motte, Geneva,
1955 (5).
Literature: Carl Einstein, *Die Kunst des 20 Jahr-
hunderts*, 1926, repr. p. 204.
Painted in 1914, it represents the Spanish artist
Iturrino and is sometimes entitled the Spanish
guitarist. Another portrait of the same sitter by
Henri Evenepoel, painted in about 1898, is in the
museum at Ghent (1898-1901).

36. THE OFFERING (*L'offrande*). Canvas, 35 × 45 in. (89 × 116 cm.). Dr. Willi Raeber, Basle.
Collection: John Quinn; Quinn sale, Hôtel Drouot, Paris, 28 October 1926 (41, repr.); Feuz, Zurich.
Exhibited: 'Derain', Kunsthalle, Berne, 1935 (36); 'Les Maîtres de l'Art Indépendant', Petit Palais, Paris, 1937 (21); 'Memorial', Paris, 1954-1955 (33, plate IX).
Literature: Adolphe Basler, *Derain* (Druet), 1929, plate 3 (as 1913); Florent Fels, *L'Art Vivant*, I, 1950, repr. p. 178.
Painted in 1913. It indicates Derain's interest in African sculpture.

37. THE GAME-BAG (*La Gibecière*). Canvas, 45 11/16 × 31 7/8 in. (116 × 81 cm.). Mme Jean Walter, Paris.
Collections: Galerie Kahnweiler, Paris (No. 2112); D. H. Kahnweiler sale, Paris, Hôtel Drouot, 13-14 June 1921 (43, repr.); Pellerin sale, Paris, Hôtel Drouot, 7 May 1926 (8, repr.).
Exhibited: 'Memorial', Paris, 1954-1955 (31); 'Derain', Galerie Maeght, Paris, 1958.
Literature: Daniel Henry, *Derain*, 1920, plate 20. Painted in 1913.

38. VIEW OF MARTIGUES (*Martigues*). Canvas, 55½ × 35 7/16 in. (141 × 90 cm.). The Hermitage, Leningrad.
Signed.
Collection: Galerie Kahnweiler, Paris (No. 2170); Stouchkine.
Literature: Les Soirées de Paris, 15 February 1914 (21), repr. p. 91; *L'Amour de l'Art*, vi, 1925, repr. p. 487; Elie Faure, *Derain*, 1923, plate 4; René Huyghe, 'Le Fauvisme: Le Reveil des Traditions', *L'Amour de l'Art*, xiv, 1933, p. 156, Fig. 193; C. Zervos, *Histoire de l'Art Contemporain*, 1938, repr. p. 179. Painted at Martigues in 1913.

39. THE TWO SISTERS (*Les Deux Soeurs*). Canvas, 77 × 51 3/8 in. (195,5 × 130,5 cm.). Statens Museum, Copenhagen.
Signed on reverse.
Collections: Galerie Kahnweiler, Paris (No. 2221); D. H. Kahnweiler sale, Paris, 7-8 May 1923 (177), bought J. Rump.
Exhibited: Grønningens Udstilling, Copenhagen, 1924 (22).
Literature: Carlo Carrà, *Derain*, 1921, Fig. 7; Carl Kjersmeir in *L'Amour de l'Art*, x, 1929, repr. p. 165; Leo Swane in *Kunstmuseet Aarskrift*, xvi-xviii, 1929-1931, p. 64, 76; Leo Swane in *Tilskueren*, 1931, I, p. 428; Leo Swane in *Kunstmuseet Aarskrift*, xx-xxi,

1933-34, p. 84; René Huyghe, *Histoire de l'Art Contemporain*, 1933-1934, repr. p. 164; *Konstrevy*, xi, 1935, repr. p. 34; M. Peschcke, *Køedt Statusopgørelse i Malerkunsten*, 1935, p. 105; Erik Zahle, *Fransk Malerei efter 1900*, 1938, p. 9, 15, plate 14; M. Raynal, A. Rudlinger, H. Bolliger, J. Lassaigne, *Histoire de la Peinture Moderne*, 1950, p. 66, 133, repr. p. 67 in colour; Werner Haftmann, *Malerei im 20 Jahrhundert*, 1955, plate 231; Denys Sutton, 'André Derain: Art as Fate', in *Encounter*, October 1955, repr. p. 72; *Statens Museum, Moderne Udelansk Kunst*, ed. Hanne Finsen, 1958 (23, repr.).
Painted in 1914. The two models were Italian girls whom Derain painted on a number of occasions. A smaller related composition is in a London private collection; see 'Derain', London, 1957 (25, repr.).

40. THE LAST SUPPER (*La Cène*). Canvas, 86 5/8 × 110¼ in. (220 × 280 cm.). The Art Institute, Chicago.
Collection: Mrs. Frank R. Lillie, Chicago.
Exhibited: 'Twentieth Century Masterpieces', Tate Gallery, London, 1952 (18).
Literature: A. Ozenfant and Jeannerat, *La Peinture Moderne*, 1925, repr. p. 51; Adolphe Basler, *Derain* (Druet), 1929, repr. p. 1 (as being in a chapel at Chicago); Carl Einstein, *Die Kunst des 20 Jahrhunderts*, 1926, repr. p. 203; Pierre Courthion, *Panorama de la Peinture Française contemporaine*, 1927, repr. opp. p. 97; André Salmon, *André Derain*, 1929, plate I; C. J. Bulliet, *The Significant Moderns*, 1936, Fig. 162; D. Tselos, 'Derain and Medievalism' in *Parnassus*, x, March 1938, pp. 7-10, repr. p. 10; R. Escholier, *La Peinture Française XX Siècle*, 1937, repr. p. 50; Florent Fels, *L'Art Vivant*, I, 1950, repr. p. 174 (as 1911).
Painted in 1913. According to Florent Fels (op. cit. p. 177), this was sold at the end of World War I for 4,000 francs. An analysis of the iconography is given by Tselos, op. cit., pp. 7-10. Derain painted biblical subjects on earlier occasions, *e.g.* a picture exhibited 'Twentieth Century Masters', Marlborough Galleries, London, 1955 (9, repr.).

41. THE DRINKERS (*Les Buveurs*). Canvas, 55⅛ × 34 5/8 in. (140 × 88 cm.). Kabutoya Gallery, Tokyo.
Signed lower right.
Collections: Galerie Kahnweiler, Paris; Paul Rosenberg.
Exhibited: 'Derain', Kunsthalle, Berne, 1935 (39); 'Les Maîtres de l'Art Indépendant', Petit Palais, Paris, 1937 (4); '50 Ans d'Art Moderne', Palais International des Beaux-Arts, Brussels, 1958 (73, as *Le billard*, 1913, plate 44).

Literature: Adolphe Basler, *Derain* (Druet), 1929, plate I; André Salmon, *Derain*, 1929, plate 4; Jean Cassou, 'Derain' in *Cahiers d'Art*, October 1926, repr. p. 190; René Huyghe, 'Le Fauvisme: Le Reveil des Traditions' in *L'Amour de l'Art*, xiv, 1933, Fig. 192 (as 1914); D. Tselos, 'Derain and Medievalism' in *Parnassus*, X, March 1938, pp. 7-10, repr. p. 8. Painted 1913-1914.

42. SATURDAY (*Le Samedi*). Canvas, 71 × 82 in. (181 × 228 cm.). The Soviet State Collection.
Collections: Galerie Kahnweiler, Paris (No. 2197); Stouchkine, Moscow.
Literature: Les Soirées de Paris, 15 February 1914 (21), repr. p. 109; Daniel Henry, *Derain*, 1920, plate 29; M. Raynal, 'André Derain' in *L'Esprit Nouveau*, 1921, repr. p. 887; André Salmon, *Derain*, 1923, repr. p. 43; Carlo Carrà, *Derain*, 1924, Fig. 18 (dated 1909-1914); *L'Amour de l'Art*, 1925, repr. p. 486; *Cicerone*, xviii, 1926, repr. p. 126; Carl Einstein, *Die Kunst des 20 Jahrhunderts*, 1926, repr. p. 202; *Pour ou contre André Derain (Les Chroniques du Jour)*, 1931, plate 5; Waldemar George, 'André Derain' in *L'Amour de l'Art*, xiv, 1933, p. 158, Fig. 194; C. Zervos, *Histoire de l'Art Contemporain*, 1938, repr. p. 179; R. H. Wilenski, *Modern French Painters*, 1940, repr. p. 70.
Painted between 1911 and 1914. The title was given to the picture by Guillaume Apollinaire.

43. 'CHEVALIER X'. Canvas, 64$\frac{3}{16}$ × 38$\frac{3}{16}$ in. (163 × 97 cm.). The Hermitage, Leningrad.
Collections: Galerie Kahnweiler, Paris (No. 2196); Stouchkine, Moscow.
Painted in 1914. According to Monsieur D. H. Kahnweiler, Derain executed the figure first and pinned a newspaper on to the canvas, which was painted in later on. For the earlier and different version, see Carlo Carrà, *Derain*, 1924, Fig. 6. The title was given to the picture by Guillaume Apollinaire.

44. STILL LIFE IN FRONT OF A WINDOW (*Nature morte devant la fenêtre*). Canvas, 50$\frac{3}{8}$ × 31$\frac{1}{8}$ in. (128 × 79 cm.). The Soviet State Collection.
Signed.
Collections: Galerie Kahnweiler, Paris (No. 2111); Stouchkine, Moscow.
Literature: André Salmon, *Derain*, 1923, repr. p. 31; Carlo Carrà, *Derain*, 1924, Fig. 29; C. Zervos, *Histoire de l'Art Contemporain*, 1938, repr. p. 180.
According to Madame Alice Derain, this was painted at Cahors in 1912.

45. HEAD OF A GIRL (*Tête de jeune fille*). Canvas. Monsieur R. Hauert, Paris.
Signed lower right.
Collection: Lucien Descaves.
Literature: André Salmon, *Derain*, 1923, repr. p. 45. Painted in 1920.

46. THE ARTIST IN HIS STUDIO (*L'Artiste et sa famille*). Canvas, 45$\frac{3}{4}$ × 35 in. (116 × 89 cm.). Pierre Matisse Gallery, New York.
Signed lower right.
Exhibited: 'Fifty Years of Portraits', Leicester Galleries, London, 1935 (92, repr. as 1914).
According to Madame Derain, it was painted in 1920-1921. Madame Derain is shown in the background and a servant in the foreground.

47. THE ITALIAN MODEL (*L'Italienne*). Canvas laid down on board, 36 × 29 in. (91,5 × 73,6 cm.). The Walker Art Gallery, Liverpool.
Collections: Valentine Gallery, New York; Hirshorn-Barbee sale, Parke Bernet, New York, 10 November 1948 (54, repr.); James Magee; The Mayor Gallery, London.
Literature: John Jacobs, *Bulletin of the Walker Art Gallery, Liverpool*, VII (3), 1958-59, pp. 3-4, repr. on cover.
Almost certainly painted in 1921-1922 after Derain's visit to Rome. The model wears Roman peasant costume; Madame Alice Derain is of the opinion that it was painted in Derain's studio in the Rue Bonaparte. The debt to Corot's *Femme au Perle* in the Louvre and his other figure paintings is clear. A head and shoulders of a girl, wearing a not dissimilar headdress, is or was in the E. Farot collection; see the *Burlington Magazine*, xxxvi, p. 311, repr. Fig. I-A.

48. THE ROAD AT ALBANO (*La Route d'Albano*). Canvas, 24$\frac{7}{16}$ × 19$\frac{11}{16}$ in. (62 × 50 cm.). Private collection, Paris.
Signed lower right.
Collection: G. K. Paris.
Literature: André Salmon, *Derain*, 1923, repr. p. 51; *The Studio*, July 1958, repr. p. 12.
Painted in Rome in 1921. For a related composition see Carlo Carrà, *Derain*, 1924, Fig. 14.

49. A VILLAGE IN PROVENCE (*Un Village Provençal*). Canvas, 31$\frac{3}{4}$ × 25$\frac{3}{4}$ in. (86 × 65,4 cm.). Mr. Peter van den Berg, New Rochelle, New York.
Signed lower right.
Collections: James Bomford; E. J. Van Wisselingh, Amsterdam.

Exhibited: 'Paintings of the French School, Bomford Collection', Arts Council, 1945 (27, plate 23).
Painted about 1921-1922.

50. NEAR CASTELGANDOLFO. Canvas, 12½×15 in. (32×38 cm.). O. Bateman-Brown, Esq.
Signed lower right.
Collections: Paul Guillaume and Brandon Davies; Reid and Lefevre, London.
Exhibited: 'Paintings from North East Homes', Aberdeen Art Gallery, 1951.
Painted in 1921.

51. WOODLAND SCENE AT OLLIOULES NEAR TOULON (*Les Arbres à Ollioules près de Toulon*). Canvas, 22×25 in. (55,9×63,5 cm.). The Earl of Sandwich.
Signed lower right.
Exhibited: Norwich Art Gallery, 1926; Contemporary Art Society, London, 1927; 'French Modern Art', Royal West of England Academy, Bristol, 1930 (26); 'Derain', London, 1957 (43).
Painted in 1921-1922 and acquired direct from the artist by Lord Sandwich shortly after it was executed.

52. FLOWER PIECE (*Un Vase de Fleurs*). Canvas, 24×36⅝ in. (61×93 cm.). Dr. Fritz Nathan, Zurich.
Collections: Matthiesen Galleries, London; Hirschland, Essen.
Exhibited: Matthiesen Galleries, London, 1938 (83, repr.).
Painted about 1924.

53. THE LADEN TABLE (*La Table Garnie*). Canvas, 38¼×64¼ in. (97,1×163,2 cm.). Mr. and Mrs. Hubert Simon, London.
Signed lower right.
Collections: State Museum, Vienna, 1924; Galerie Simon, Paris, 1925; Mrs. R. A. Workman, 1925; Bignou Gallery, New York; Mrs. S. Kaye, 1944; Messrs. Reid and Lefevre, London.
Exhibited: Alfred Flechtheim Galerie, Berlin, 1922; at the Dusseldorf Museum, 1927; 'Works by Derain', Knoedler Galleries, New York, 1930 (5, repr.); 'Cent ans de Peinture Française', Galerie Georges Petit, Paris, 1930 (5, repr.); 'Derain', Art Museum, Cincinnati, 1930-1 (39, repr.); 'L'Ecole de Paris', Lefevre Gallery, London, 1932 (4, repr.); 'Tentoonstelling van Fransche Schilderkunst, Ecole de Paris', Stedelijk Museum, Amsterdam, 1932 (60); 'Het Stilleven', Jacques Goudstikker, Amsterdam, 1933 (80); 'Derain', Brummer Gallery, New York, 1936 (41), lent by Bignou Gallery; Detroit Institute of Arts (Alger House), Grosse Pointe, Michigan,

1936; 'The School of Paris', Montreal, 1936 (4, repr.); 'L'Ecole de Paris', The Lefevre Gallery, London, 1938 (11, repr.); 'Picasso and his Contemporaries', Messrs. Reid and Lefevre, London, 1943 (6); 'Four Centuries of Still Life in France', Boymans Museum, Rotterdam, 1954 (139, repr.); 'Memorial', Paris, 1954-5 (40); 'Derain', London, 1957 (40, repr.); 'The Dial', Worcester Art Museum, 1959 (27).
Literature: Paul Westheim, 'Die Kunst in Frankreich', in *Das Kunstblatt*, January 1922, repr. p. 11; Georg Biermann, 'Neue Arbeiten von André Derain' in *Cicerone*, 1923, repr. p. 218 (as 1922); *Kunst und Künstler*, XXI, (1922-3), repr. p. 146; Hans Tietze, *Die Französische Malerei der Gegenwart*, 1925, plate 15; Hans Tietze, *Lebendige Kunstwissenschaft*, 1925, repr. p. 90; Carl Einstein, *Die Kunst des 20 Jahrhunderts*, 1926, repr. p. 126; *The Dial*, lxxxiii (1927), p. 91 (repr. in colour); *Art News*, No. 27, April 1930, p. 5, repr.; S. C. Kaines Smith, *The Painters of France*, 1932, plate 15, p. 72; *The Connoisseur*, xlix, January 1937, p. 42; *The Artist*, May 1937; *Goya, Revista de Arte* (Madrid), 1954, repr. p. 123; *Encyclopedia Britannica*, 15th ed.; Denys Sutton, 'André Derain', in *Encounter*, October 1955, repr. p. 69.
Painted in 1921 or 1922.

54. VASE OF ROSES, WITH PLATE AND PIPE (*Vase de roses, assiette et pipe*). Canvas, 7⅜×9⅝ in. (18×24 cm.). Dr. Willi Raeber, Basle.
Painted about 1923-1925.

55. THE BEAUTIFUL MODEL (*Le Beau Modèle*). Canvas, 44⅞×35⅞ in. (114×91 cm.). Private collection, Paris.
Signed lower right.
Collection: Paul Guillaume.
Exhibited: 'Derain', Charpentier, Paris, 1955 (15, repr.).
Literature: Waldemar George, *La Grande Peinture Contemporaine à la Collection Paul Guillaume*, 1929, repr. p. 83.
Painted in 1923. The technique of this picture may be compared with another painting of a nude model; repr. Waldemar George, op. cit. p. 97.

56. HARLEQUIN (*Arléquin*). Canvas, 29½×24 in. (73,6×61 cm.). National Gallery of Art, Washington, D.C. (Chester Dale Collection).
Signed lower left.
Collections: Paul Guillaume; Messrs. Reid and Lefevre, London.
Exhibited: 'André Derain', Reid and Lefevre, London, 1928 (5, as 1919); 'Cent ans de la Peinture

Française', Stedelijk Museum, Amsterdam, 1928 (5); 'Trente Ans de la Peinture Française', Brussels, 1930; 'Derain-Vlaminck', Museum of French Art, 1932 (16).
Literature: Apollo, VIII, 1928, repr. p. 174; C. Zervos, *Histoire de l'Art Contemporain*, 1938, repr. p. 183 (as 1919); *Twentieth Century French Paintings from the Chester Dale Collection*, 1952, repr. p. 20. Although often given to the year 1919, Madame Alice Derain is of the opinion that it dates from 1924. A painting of a Harlequin, apparently of 1923, is in the Statens Museum, Copenhagen; see *Moderne Udenlandsk Kunst*, ed. Hanne Finsen, 1958, p. 24.

57. NUDE WITH A CAT (*Nu au chat*). Canvas, 65⅜ × 34⅝ in. (166 × 88 cm.). Madame Charles Baron, Paris.
Signed lower right.
Collections: Messrs. Reid and Lefevre, London; Messrs. Knoedler, New York.
Exhibited: 'Derain', Knoedler, New York, 1930 (10, repr.); 'Derain', Art Museum, Cincinnati, 1930-1931 (26, repr.); 'Memorial', Paris, 1954-1955 (46).
Literature: André Basler, *Derain*, 1931, Fig. 6; Elie Faure, *Derain*, plate 26 (as 1922-1923); Malcolm Vaughan, *Derain*, 1941, repr. p. 15 in colour; Jean Leymarie, *Derain*, 1948, plate 9 in colour; Patrick Heron, 'Derain Reconsidered' in *Arts*, January 1958, repr. p. 26.
Painted between 1921-1923.

58. WOMAN IN A CHEMISE (*La Femme en chemise*). Canvas, 30½ × 23 ¹⅜ in. (77,5 × 60,5 cm.). Chester Dale Collection, New York.
Signed lower right.
Collection: Pierre Lévy, Troyes.
Literature: Twentieth Century French Paintings from the Chester Dale Collection, 1952, repr. p. 24.
Painted about 1928. The same model appears in a picture, *The Sleeper*, once in the Paul Guillaume collection, Paris.

59. PORTRAIT OF VINCENT MUSELLI (*Portrait de Vincent Muselli*). Canvas, 24 × 19 ¹¹⁄₁₆ in. (61 × 50 cm.). Madame Fernand Halphen, Paris.
Signed lower right and dedicated to Vincent Muselli.
Collection: Vautheret, sale, Paris, Hôtel Drouot, 16 June 1933 (6 repr.).
Exhibited: 'Memorial', Paris, 1954-1955 (59).
Literature: Waldemar George, 'Derain', in *L'Amour de l'Art*, xiv, 1933, repr. p. 161 (as 1926).
Painted in 1925. A portrait drawing of Muselli is repr. in André Salmon, *Derain*, 1929, p. 46.

60. HARLEQUIN (*Arléquin*). Chalk on paper, 19 ¹¹⁄₁₆ × 13⅜ in. (50 × 34 cm.). Monsieur Pierre Lévy, Troyes.
Signed lower right and inscribed *A Paul Guillaume*.
Collection: Paul Guillaume.
Exhibited: 'Cent cinquante ans de dessins', Galerie Bernheim-Jeune, Paris, 1952-53; 'Le Dessin de Toulouse Lautrec aux Cubistes', Musée d'Art Moderne, Paris, 1954 (36).
Literature: Du, October 1956, repr. p. 38.
A study for the Harlequin in No. 61.

61. PIERROT AND HARLEQUIN (*Pierrot et Arléquin*). Canvas, 69 ⁵⁄₁₆ × 69 ⁵⁄₁₆ in. (176 × 176 cm.). Madame Jean Walter, Paris.
Signed on right.
Collection: Paul Guillaume.
Exhibited: 'Memorial', Paris, 1954-1955 (51 repr., plate XII).
Literature: Jean Cassou, 'Derain' in *Cahiers d'Art*, October 1926, repr. p. 197; *Drawing and Design*, 1927, repr. p. 164; Waldemar George, *La Grande Peinture Contemporaine à la collection Paul Guillaume*, 1929, repr. p. 109; Waldemar George, 'André Derain', in *L'Amour de l'Art*, xiv, 1933, repr. p. 160; René Huyghe, *Les Contemporains*, 1939, plate 50; *La Renaissance*, March 1939 (in colour); Francis Carco, *L'Ami du Peintre*, 1944, p. 103.
Painted in 1924. From the account of this picture given by Francis Carco (op. cit. p. 103), it seems as if it was commissioned by Paul Guillaume. According to Waldemar George (op. cit. p. 163) the theme was inspired by an engraving of a scene from the Commedia dell'Arte. The subject matter certainly reflects Derain's interest in the theatre which found expression in his designs for the Ballet and the Opera which started in 1919 when he executed the costumes and sets for *La Boutique Fantasque*, first performed in that year by Diaghileff's company: see pp. 34-35, 158.
A small oil sketch for the picture is in the collection of Lord Radcliffe: see 'Derain', London, 1947 (47). A drawing for Harlequin is in the Pierre Lévy collection, Troyes (see Fig. 60). A half-length study of *Harlequin* is in the Chester Dale collection, Washington, D.C. (Fig. 56); a figure of *Harlequin holding a Guitar* belongs to Madame Jean Walter (Fig. 64); another Harlequin is in the Statens Museum, Copenhagen.

62. THE KITCHEN TABLE (*La Table de Cuisine*). Canvas, 47¼ × 47¼ in. (120 × 120 cm.). Madame Jean Walter, Paris.
Signed lower right.
Collection: Paul Guillaume.

Exhibited: 'Derain', Brummer Gallery, New York, 1936 (1); 'Les Maîtres de l'Art Indépendant', Petit Palais, Paris, 1937 (28); 'The Art of the Third Republic', Worcester Art Museum, 1941; 'Memorial', Paris, 1954-1955 (53).
Literature: Maurice Raynal, *Anthologie de la Peinture en France de 1906 à Nos Jours*, 1927, repr. p. 121; *Drawing and Design*, iv, 1928, repr. p. 280; A. Basler, *Derain* (Druet), 1929, plate 9; Waldemar George, *La Grande Peinture Contemporaine à la Collection Paul Guillaume*, 1929, repr. p. 105; André Salmon, *Derain*, 1929, plate 11.
Painted in 1924. This major work indicates that Derain had studied the painting of the Caravaggesque masters.

63. STILL LIFE: DEAD GAME (*Nature Morte: La Chasse*). Canvas, 77 × 52 in. (196 × 132 cm.). The Carnegie Institute, Pittsburgh.
Exhibited: 'Derain', Cincinnati Art Museum, 1930-1931 (37, repr.); 'Derain', Brummer Gallery, New York, 1936 (39); 'Les Maîtres de l'Art Indépendant', 1895-1937, Petit Palais, Paris, 1937 (23).
Literature: *Art Digest*, iii, 1928, repr.
Painted about 1918. It won the 1928 Carnegie Prize.

64. HARLEQUIN WITH A GUITAR (*Arléquin à la Guitare*). Canvas, 74 13/16 × 37 7/16 in. (190 × 95 cm.). Madame Jean Walter, Paris.
Collection: Paul Guillaume.
Exhibited: 'Derain', Galerie Charpentier, Paris, 1955 (23); 'Derain', Galerie Maeght, Paris, 1958 (4, repr. in colour on cover).
Literature: Adolphe Basler, *Derain*, 1931, repr. (on cover); Waldemar George, *La Grande Peinture contemporaine à la collection Paul Guillaume*, 1929, repr. p. 33.
Painted in 1924. It is related to Figs. 56, 60, 61.

65. THE LARGE NUDE (*Grand Nu*). Canvas, 36¼ × 28¾ in. (92 × 73 cm.). Monsieur Max Moos, Geneva.
Signed lower right.
Collection: Zborowski, anon. sale, Paris, Hôtel Drouot, 17 March 1928 (18, repr.).
Exhibited: 'Memorial', Paris, 1954-1955 (71).
Literature: *The Studio*, February 1955, repr. p. 89; Waldemar George, 'Derain peintre de l'intemperel' in *Prisme des Arts*, No. 13, 1957, repr. p. 24.
Painted in about 1928-1929. A painting of what seems to be the same model was once in the Ozuski Collection; see *L'Art Vivant*, vi, 1930, Fig. 22.

66. GENEVIÈVE (*Geneviève*). Canvas, 39¾ × 30 in. (110 × 76 cm.). Madame Jean Walter, Paris.

Signed lower right.
Collection: Paul Guillaume.
Exhibited: 'Derain', Brummer Gallery, New York, 1936 (2); 'Derain', Galerie Maeght, Paris, 1958 (2).
Literature: W. George in *Formes*, xxxi, 1933, repr. opp. p. 340.
Painted in 1931. The sitter is Derain's niece, Geneviève.

67. THE BLONDE ITALIAN (*L'Italienne blonde*). Canvas, 26¾ × 28¾ in. (92 × 73 cm.). Madame Jean Walter, Paris.
Signed lower right.
Collection: Paul Guillaume, Paris.
Exhibited: 'Derain', Galerie Charpentier, Paris, 1955 (30, repr. as 1934); 'Derain', Galerie Maeght, Paris, 1958 (14, as 1925).
The style of the picture and the appearance of the sitter would suggest that it dates from the 1930's rather than from the previous decade.

68. THE BASILICA OF ST MAXIMIN (*La Basilique de St. Maximin*). Chalk on paper, 9 13/16 × 15¾ in. (25 × 40 cm.). Monsieur Pierre Lévy, Troyes.
Signed on left.
Exhibited: 'Le Dessin de Toulouse Lautrec aux Cubistes', Musée d'Art Moderne, Paris, 1954 (37).
A preliminary study for No. 69.

69. THE BASILICA OF ST MAXIMIN (*La Basilique de St. Maximin*). Canvas, 23⅝ × 28¾ in. (60 × 73 cm.). Musée National d'Art Moderne, Paris.
Signed lower right.
Literature: J. Cassou—B. Dorival, *Musée National d'Art Moderne: Catalogue-Guide*, 1947, p. 23.
Painted in 1930. Acquired by the French State in 1933. A drawing for the composition is in the collection of Monsieur Pierre Lévy, Troyes: see Fig. 68.

70. THE FOUNTAIN AT OLIÈRES (*La Fontaine d'Olières*). Canvas, 36¼ × 28¾ in. (92 × 73 cm.). Madame Jean Walter, Paris.
Signed lower right.
Collection: Paul Guillaume, Paris.
Exhibited: 'Memorial', Paris, 1954-1955 (75); 'Derain', Galerie Maeght, Paris, 1958 (12).
Literature: Adolphe Basler, *Derain*, 1931, Fig. 31 (as *Environs de Saint Maximin*).
Painted in 1930. A view of the same view from a rather different angle is reproduced by Jacques Guenne 'L'Art d'André Derain' in *L'Art Vivant*, May 1931, p. 205. Another view, formerly with the Lilienfeld Gallery, New York, is reproduced by Malcolm Vaughan, *Derain*, 1941, p. 24 (as 1910).

71. THE GLADE (*La Clairière*). Canvas, 19⅓₆ × 24⅝ in. (50 × 62 cm.). Madame Jean Walter, Paris.
Signed lower right.
Collection: Paul Guillaume, Paris.
Exhibited: 'Derain', Galerie Maeght, Paris, 1958 (25, repr. in colour).
Painted in 1931.

72. TWO NUDES WITH FRUIT (*Deux Nus aux fruits*). Canvas, 44⅛ × 41 in. (112 × 104 cm.). Monsieur Pierre Lévy, Troyes.
Signed lower right.
Exhibited: 'Cinquante ans de la Peinture française dans les collections particulières', Musée des Arts Décoratifs, Paris, 1952 (46, plate 19); 'Figures nudes d'Ecole Française depuis les maîtres de Fontainebleau', Galerie Charpentier, Paris, 1953 (5); 'Derain', Biennale, Venice, 1954 (6); 'Derain', Galerie Charpentier, 1955 (34). Derain, Geneva, (1959, 39).
Literature: Les Arts, 21 March 1952; Waldemar George, 'Derain peintre de l'intemperel' in *Prisme des Arts*, No. 13, 1957, repr. p. 27.
Painted about 1935.

73. THE SURPRISE (*La Surprise*). Canvas. 55 × 120½ in. (140 × 306 cm.). Mrs. Averill Harriman, New York.
Collection: Marie Harriman Gallery, New York.
Exhibited: 'Paintings from Private Collection', Metropolitan Museum, New York, 1903 (34).
Literature: Malcolm Vaughan, *Derain*, 1941, repr. p. 21.
Painted in 1938.

74. THE STAG HUNT (*La Chasse aux Cerfs*.). Canvas, 78 × 63¼ in. (198 × 161 cm.). From 1938 to 1957 in the Winterbotham Collection of the Chicago Art Institute.
Signed lower right.
Exhibited: Pittsburgh, Carnegie International, Oct.-Dec. 1939.
Literature: F. A. Sweet in: *Bulletin of the Art Institute, Chicago*, XXXIII, Sept.-Oct. 1939, pp. 74-75, repr. on cover; *Art Digest*, XIV, 15 October 1939, p. 8; *L'Amour de l'Art*, VI, (special no.), July 1946, p. 180; *Chicago Art Institute, The Winterbotham Collection*, Chicago, 1947, p. 15.
Painted about 1938. Copied in Aubusson tapestry.

75. THE PAINTER WITH HIS FAMILY (*Le Peintre et sa Famille*). Canvas, 68½ × 48⅞ in. (174 × 124 cm.).
Private collection, Paris.
Signed lower right.

Exhibited: 'Derain', Pierre Matisse, New York, 1941 (2); 'Memorial', Paris, 1954-1955 (91).
Literature: Malcolm Vaughan, *Derain*, 1941, repr. p. 43 in colour (as 1940).
Painted about 1939. This picture indicates Derain's interest in Pompeian art, Caravaggism, Egyptian portraiture and Flemish painting.

76. THE DRUMMER BOY (*L'Enfant au Tambour*). Canvas, 36¼ × 28¾ in. (92 × 73 cm.). Private collection, Paris.
Exhibited: 'Memorial', Paris, 1954-1955 (96); Musée de Grenoble, 1956; 'Derain', London, 1957 (69). 'Derain', Geneva, 1959 (48).
Painted in 1945. The sitter is Derain's son André. For another portrait of him, painted in 1942, see 'Derain', London, 1957 (68, repr.).

77. THE DEPORTEE (*La Deportée*). Panel, 15¾ × 11¼ in. (40 × 28,5 cm.). Monsieur Pierre Lévy, Troyes.
Signed lower right.
Exhibited: 'Derain', Geneva, 1959 (77).
Painted about 1941. Another picture with a related theme— *The Belgian Refugee*, of 1941—is in the collection of Monsieur N. Mazaraki, Vence, Alpes-Maritimes: see 'Memorial', Paris, 1954-1955 (93).

78. FLOWERS IN A VASE (*Fleurs dans un Vase*). Canvas, 29½ × 37½ in. (75 × 95,3 cm.). National Gallery of Art, Washington, D.C. (Chester Dale Collection).
Signed lower right.
Exhibited: 'Flowers by French Painters, XIX - XX Centuries', Messrs. Knoedler, New York, 1932 (23); 'Flowers in Art', Pennsylvania Museum, Philadelphia, 1933.
Literature: Malcolm Vaughan, *Derain*, 1941, repr. p. 41; *Twentieth Century French Paintings from the Chester Dale Collection*, 1952, p. 25.
Painted in 1932.

79. STILL LIFE (*Nature Morte*). Canvas, 37⅞ × 51⅛ in. (95 × 130 cm.). Monsieur Pierre Lévy, Troyes.
Exhibited: 'La Pain et la Vie', Galerie Charpentier, Paris, 1954 (42); 'La Nature Morte Française', Boymans Museum, Rotterdam, 1954 (140); 'Derain', Galerie Charpentier, Paris, 1955 (35).
Literature: Connaissance des Arts, May 1954, repr. p. 70; *Plaisirs de France*, June 1954, repr. p. 69.
Painted in 1938-1939.

80. STILL LIFE WITH FRUIT AND FLOWERS (*Nature morte aux fruits et feuillages*). Canvas, 44⅞ × 56⁵⁄₁₆ in. (114 × 143 cm.). Monsieur Pierre Lévy, Troyes.

Exhibited: 'Cinquante ans de Peinture française dans les collections particulières', Musée des Arts Décoratifs, Paris, 1952 (47); 'Derain', Biennale, Venice, 1954 (3); 'Derain', Galerie Charpentier, Paris, 1955 (53, repr.).
Painted about 1945.

81. STILL LIFE ON BLACK GROUND (*Nature morte fond noir*). Canvas, 38 3/16 × 51 3/16 in. (97 × 130 cm.). Monsieur Pierre Lévy, Troyes.
Exhibited: Le Salon de Tuileries, Paris, 1952 (58, repr.); 'Derain', Biennale, Venice, 1954 (1); 'Derain', Galerie Charpentier, Paris, 1955 (55, repr.); 'Cent Chefs d'oeuvres de l'art français, 1750-1950', Galerie Charpentier, Paris, 1957 (26, repr.).
Literature: Elle, 18 October 1954, p. 21; *Nouveau Femina*, November 1954; *Figaro*, 22 April 1955; *Paris Match*, 4 June 1955, p. 22; *Du*, October 1956, repr. p. 33; Waldemar George, 'Derain peintre de l'intemperel' in *Prisme des Arts*, No. 13, 1957, repr. p. 26.
Painted about 1945.

82. LANDSCAPE ON THE BANKS OF THE LOIRE AT OUSSON (*Paysage sur les bords de la Loire, à Ousson*). Canvas, 25 5/8 × 36 1/4 in. (65 × 92 cm.). Monsieur Pierre Lévy, Troyes.
Signed lower right.
Exhibited: Oslo; 'Les Amis de Metthey', Galerie de L'Elysée, Paris, June 1950; 'Présence de la Nature', Galerie Bernier, Paris, 1950; 'Derain', Galerie Charpentier, Paris, 1955 (45, repr.); 'Derain', London, 1957 (67, repr.). 'Derain', Geneva, 1959 (70).
Literature: Les Arts, 8 December 1950.
Painted about 1942.

83. THE TWO SHEDS (*Les deux Hangars*). Canvas, 31 1/2 × 39 in. (80 × 99 cm.). Monsieur Pierre Lévy, Troyes.
Signed lower right.
Exhibited: 'Derain', XXVII Biennale, Venice, 1954 (2); Cultural Centre, Rome, 1954; 'Derain', Galerie Charpentier, Paris, 1955 (47, repr.); 'Derain', Salon d'Asnières, Paris, 1958 (11); 'Derain', Geneva, 1959 (79).
Literature: Du, October 1956, repr. p. 31; *Le Peintre*, 15 October 1958, repr. p. 13.
Painted in Touraine in about 1943. A smaller painting of the same scene is in the Pierre Lévy collection, Troyes: see 'Derain', Salon d'Asnières, 1958 (10). Another painting, 'The Thatched Shed in Touraine', is also in the same collection: see 'Derain', Salon d'Asnières, 1958 (14, repr.).

84. AMIENS. Canvas, 35 7/16 × 42 15/16 in. (90 × 109 cm.). Monsieur Pierre Lévy, Troyes.
Signed lower right.
Exhibited: 'Derain', Biennale, Venice, 1954 (5); Cultural Centre, Rome; 'Memorial', Paris, 1954-1955 (99, repr., plate XVI); 'Derain', Galerie Charpentier, Paris, 1955 (50). 'Derain', Geneva, 1959 (70, repr.).
Literature: Arts, 8 December 1950. *Rivarol*, 30 December 1954.
Painted about 1946.

85. BOATS AT NOIRMOUTIER (*Bateaux à Noirmoutier*). Canvas, 18 1/8 × 13 in. (46 × 33 cm.). Monsieur Pierre Lévy, Troyes.
Signed lower right.
Exhibited: 'Plaisirs de France', Galerie Charpentier, Paris, 1951 (45); 'Derain', Galerie Charpentier, Paris, 1955 (57). 'Derain', Geneva, 1959 (53).
Painted in 1950.

86. THE OPPRESSIVE LANDSCAPE (*Paysage Triste*). Canvas, 14 1/4 × 15 3/4 in. (36 × 40 cm.). Monsieur Pierre Lévy, Troyes.
Exhibited: 'Paysage de l'Ile de France', Versailles.
Painted about 1946. A related picture, 'The Sinister Landscape', is in the Lévy collection.

87. BACCHANTES (*Les Bacchantes*). Canvas, 19 11/16 × 24 in. (50 × 61 cm.). Monsieur Pierre Lévy, Troyes.
Exhibited: 'Derain', Salon d'Asnières, 1958 (16).
Literature: L'Amateur d'Art, 10 October 1958, repr. on cover.
One of a group of sketches painted in about 1945. This includes the *Embarquement pour Cythère*, and *Nudes against Trees* (repr. in *Le Nouveau Femina*, November, 1954), both in the Pierre Lévy collection, Troyes.

88. A DESIGN FOR MAM'ZELLE ANGOT (*Un décor pour Mam'zelle Angot*). Madame Alice Derain, Chambourcy.
Exhibited: 'Derain', London, 1957 (71, repr.).
Front cloth for a short scene between Scene I and Scene II.
Derain designed the sets for the first London production of this ballet (music after Alexandre Charles Lecocq, orchestrated by Gordon Jacob: choreography by Leonard Massine) which was performed by the Sadlers Wells (now The Royal Ballet) at Covent Garden Theatre on 26 November 1947. (This ballet was first produced with settings by Mitislav Dobuzhinsky by the Ballet Theatre in New York in October 1945.)

ILLUSTRATIONS IN THE TEXT

Frontispiece.

SELF PORTRAIT (*Autoportrait*). Canvas, 21½ × 14 in. (54,6 × 35,6 cm.). Eric Estorick, Esq., London.
Collections: Paul Eluard; Adolphe Basler; Dikran Kelekian; Kelekian sale, American Art Association, New York, 30-31 January 1923 (42); J. K. Thannhauser, New York.
Exhibited: 'Derain', Kunsthalle, Berne, 1935 (23); 'Les Maîtres de l'Art Indépendant, 1895-1937', Petit Palais, Paris, 1937 (15); '20th Century Portraits', Museum of Modern Art, New York, 1942, p. 135; 'Derain, Vlaminck, Souverbie', Messrs. Roland, Browse and Delbanco, London, 1953 (9); 'Memorial', Paris, 1954-1955 (34) plate X; Tate Gallery, 1955; 'Derain', London, 1957 (27).
Literature: Florent Fels, 'Pariser Kunstchronik', in *Das Kunstblatt*, January 1920, repr. p. 299; Carl Einstein, *Die Kunst des 20 Jahrhunderts*, 1926, p. 205 (as 1918); Adolphe Basler, *Derain*, 1929, Fig. 2 (as 1913); Paul Westheim, *Künstlerbekenntnisse*, (n.d.) repr., opposite p. 152; Monroe Wheeler, *20th Century Portraits*, 1942, p. 100; Michelangelo Masciotta, *Autoritratti dal XIV Secolo al XX Secolo*, 1955, repr. p. 223; Florent Fels, *l'Art Vivant*, I, 1950, repr. p. 183.
According to the artist this portrait was painted in 1914. A *Self Portrait* in pencil of *c.* 1912 is in the collection of Monsieur Pierre Lévy: cf. *Le dessin: De Toulouse Lautrec aux Cubistes*, Musée d'Art Moderne, Paris, 1954 (34). A *Self Portrait* of about 1912 is in the Minneapolis Art Institute: see below. Giacometti based his portrait of Derain on this *Self Portrait*.

pages 4 and 159:

Three Painted Plates. Diameter 10½ in. (26 cm.). Madame Alice Derain, Chambourcy.
Exhibited: 'Memorial', Paris, 1955-1956 (151, 152, 153).
Executed about 1906 when Derain was working for André Metthey at Vollard's instigation.

facing p. 8:

SELF PORTRAIT (*Autoportrait*). Canvas, 45 × 35 in. (90 × 116 cm.). The Institute of Art, Minneapolis. Signed on reverse.
Collection: John Quinn; Quinn sale, Paris, Hôtel Drouot, 28 October 1926 (43, repr.); Fukushima; Pierre Matisse Gallery, New York; Mr. and Mrs. John Cowles (by whom presented to Institute of Art, Minneapolis).

Exhibited: 'Art in our Time', Museum of Modern Art, New York, 1939, p. 99 repr.
Literature: Forbes Watson, *John Quinn Collection*, 1926, p. 8 repr., p. 44; L. Goldscheider, *Five Hundred Self Portraits*, 1937, Fig. 474; Alfred Werner, 'The Tragedy of André Derain' in *Arts*, January, 1958, p. 23.
Painted about 1912. For another *Self Portrait*, see Frontispiece.

facing p. 9:

MADAME DERAIN IN A WHITE SHAWL (*Madame Derain au châle blanc*). Canvas, 76¾ × 37¾ in. (195 × 96 cm.). Private collection, Paris.
Exhibited: 'Derain', Charpentier, Paris, 1955 (19, repr. as 1927).
According to Madame Alice Derain, this was painted about 1919-1920. The bowl of flowers may be compared with that in the *Still Life with a Basket* of about 1919 in the collection of M. Renou, Paris: see 'Memorial', Paris, 1954-1955 (37).

p. 35:

Four designs for *La Boutique Fantasque*. (Madame Alice Derain). Each 12⅝ × 9½ in. (32 × 24 cm.).
Exhibited: 'Derain', London, 1957 (31-34).
Derain designed the curtain, setting and costumes for Diaghelieff's ballet *La Boutique Fantasque* (music by Rossini, arranged and orchestrated by Resphigi; choreography by Massine), which was first performed at the Alhambra Theatre, London, on 5 June 1919. It was the first occasion on which Derain worked for the stage. The designs illustrated here represent: *Danseuse, Danseur de Tarantelle, Danseur de Cancan, Marchand de Pastèque*.

pages 52 and 142:

Three Decorations.
Collections: Walter Halvorsen, Paris; Georges Bernheim, Paris.
Literature: Clive Bell, *Old Friends*, 1957, p. 187.
In January 1920, Derain painted a series of eleven canvases to be used as decorations for the dining room in the apartment of Walter Halvorsen at 6 Place du Palais Bourbon, Paris. He attached the empty canvases on to the wall and worked on them for about two months. The series consists of figure subjects and two friezes. They were subsequently sold to Georges Bernheim and installed in a house he was then building in Paris.

ACKNOWLEDGEMENTS

I would like to express my thanks to Madame Alice Derain, who has answered many questions and assisted me in various ways. My thanks are also due to Mr. Clive Bell; Professor George Hamilton; Monsieur D. H. Kahnweiler; Monsieur Pierre Lévy; Mr. Denis Mahon; Mr. Benedict Nicolson; Mr. Stuart Preston; Mr. John Russell; and Monsieur Georges Wildenstein; as well as to all private owners and Museum authorities who have given permission for reproduction.   D.S.